Praise for *The Cros.*

MW00667865

As a Catholic educational leader, I ⎯⎯⎯⎯⎯⎯⎯ to cultivate global
and culturally-relevant perspectives in my students. *The Cross: A Universal Symbol* is an outstanding resource for educators to incorporate
these perspectives through the lens of faith. I especially appreciated
the diverse range of beliefs it highlighted, and I found myself with a
newfound appreciation for some of the crosses identified in this book!
Excellent read!

– Jayda Pugliese, M.Ed., principal,
St. Mary Interparochial School, Philadelphia, Pennsylvania

The world is filled with crosses that range from the majestic gold
pieces topping cathedrals to the wooden memorials dotting highways. *The Cross: A Universal Symbol* explains the history and symbolism
of the variations. and gives readers greater understanding of the crosses
seen on public buildings, flags, and houses of worship.

– Grace O'Neill, Ed.D., principal emeritus,
St. Joseph School, Elkins Park, Pennsylvania

THE
CROSS

A

UNIVERSAL

SYMBOL

Helen Hoffner, Ed.D.

Available from:
Marian Helpers Center
Stockbridge, MA 01263

Prayerline: 1-800-804-3823
Orderline: 1-800-462-7426

Websites:
Marian.org
ShopMercy.org

Library of Congress Control Number: 2023935887
ISBN: 978-1-59614-584-9

Imprimi Potest:
Very Rev. Chris Alar, MIC
Provincial Superior
The Blessed Virgin Mary, Mother of Mercy Province
Sept. 14, 2023
Feast of the Exaltation of the Holy Cross

Nihil Obstat:
Robert A. Stackpole, STD
Censor Deputatus
Sept. 14, 2023

Note: The *Nihil Obstat* and corresponding *Imprimi Potest* confirm that this work contains nothing contrary to faith or morals.

Designed by Curtis Bohner

All photographs and illustrations are either public domain or taken by the author, with the exception of page 20, "The Ladder Cross," by Kathi Jogan, and page 28, "The Y Cross" by Mary Castellano. Used with permission.

MARIAN PRESS
STOCKBRIDGE   MA 01263

With gratitude to my parents, George and Gloria Hoffner, my grandmother, Helen Brady, and all of my family for their encouragement and support.

Special thanks to my colleagues at Holy Family University for sharing their expertise, time, and suggestions to enrich my work.

Contents

Introduction

While today it is the most recognizable symbol of Christianity, the cross, from the Latin *crux*, is older than the faith and has held various forms and meanings before and after the birth of Jesus Christ. Ancient Egyptians used the ankh, a cross with a loop at the top, to symbolize life. The Greek Cross traces its origins to ancient Babylon, where it represented the sun god.

Whether proclaiming a religious belief or a historical event, a cross appears on the national flags of 28 of the 193 member countries of the United Nations. Each of the United States of America has its own flag, and crosses appear on several, including Alabama, Florida, Hawaii, Maryland, Mississippi, New Mexico, and Rhode Island. The Scandinavian countries of Denmark, Finland, Iceland, and Norway are united by their use of the Nordic Cross, also known as the Scandinavian Cross.

This book will help you identify and understand the history of many of the crosses seen on historic monuments, houses of worship, flags, and anywhere your travels may lead. It also addresses many examples of crucifixes, or crosses that contain an image of the Body of Jesus Christ.

Stories of crosses awaken curiosity about medieval knights, crusades, and the exploration of new lands. Every cross has a story to tell.

CHAPTER 1

Forms and Symbols of the Cross and Crucifixion

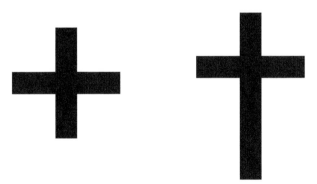

The Greek Cross and the Latin Cross

Modern crosses are usually based on either the Greek Cross or the Latin Cross. The Greek Cross, known as the *Crux Quadrata* (Cross Square), resembles the plus sign used in mathematical addition (+). Its four arms are of equal length. The Latin Cross, *Crux Immis* (Cross Sent In), has a base stem that is longer than the other three arms.

The Russian Orthodox Cross

The Russian Orthodox Cross (also known as the Eastern Orthodox Cross or the Byzantine Cross) has three bars across the base that symbolize the Crucifixion of Jesus Christ. The small top bar replicates the sign on which Pilate mockingly proclaimed, "Jesus of Nazareth, King of the Jews" (INRI). The wider bar across the middle is a remembrance that Jesus' arms were nailed to the cross. The final bar at the bottom represents the footstool on which rested Jesus' feet.

Cross with a Circle

A Latin Cross with a circle in the middle is often seen in Christian churches. For Christians, the circle represents everlasting love as well as the hope of eternal life with God in Heaven.

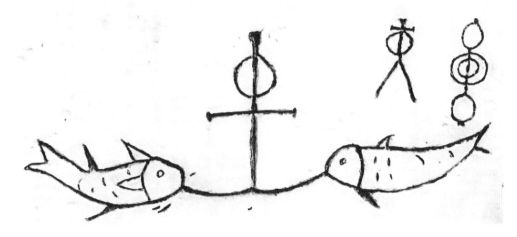

Fish and Anchors:
Early Symbols of Christianity

Today, the cross is associated with the Christian faith. The first followers of Jesus Christ, however, used fish and anchors as their symbols.

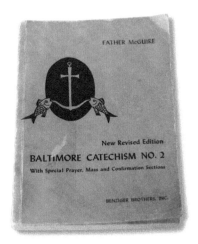

The 1960 edition of *The Baltimore Catechism*, a classic textbook that Catholic school children used to learn their faith, had an image of two fish and an anchor on the cover. The text explained,

> The early Christians used the fish to represent Christ, because the Greek word for fish, *Ichthus*, contains the first letter from each of the Greek words for Jesus, Christ, God, Son, Savior. Sometimes, the early Christians used smaller fish to represent the faithful, for they were regarded as little Christs. The early Christian writer Tertullian said, "We little fishes are born in water after the example of Jesus Christ our fish (Baptism)."[1]

Christ often referred to fish when He was teaching. "As he was walking by the sea of Galilee, he saw two brothers, Simon, who is called Peter, and his brother Andrew, casting a net into the sea (for they were fishermen). He said to them, 'Come after me, and I will make you fishers of men'" (Mt 4:18 – 19).

Saint Luke's Gospel tells of the miracle of Jesus feeding thousands with bread and fish: "Then taking the five loaves and the two fish, and looking up to heaven, he said the blessing over them, broke them, and gave them to the disciples to set before the crowd. They all ate and were satisfied. And when the leftover fragments were picked up, they filled twelve wicker baskets" (Lk 9:16 – 17).

During times when Christians were persecuted, a fish served as a secret symbol of the faith and enabled Christians to communicate with each other. Wearing or displaying a simple drawing of a fish let fellow believers know that you were a Christian.

The anchors, according to *The Baltimore Catechism*, "represented the hope of salvation through Christ's redemption of man by His death on the cross. In the figure of the anchor we see a veiled reference to the cross, and just as anchors keep boats from drifting, so hope anchors us to faith."[2] Early Christian tombs sometimes had an anchor inscribed to symbolize safety and hope in a future life with Christ. Hebrews 6:19 – 20 states, "This we have as an anchor of the soul, sure and firm, which reaches into the interior behind the veil, where Jesus has entered on our behalf as forerunner, becoming high priest forever according to the order of Melchizedek."

The Yoke

> "Come to me, all you who labor and are burdened, and I will give you rest. Take my yoke upon you and learn from me, for I am meek and humble of heart; and you will find rest for yourselves. For my yoke is easy, and my burden light." (Mt 11:28 – 30)

When there is a burden to be carried, we seek solutions to lighten the load. Since the earliest days, workers have carried heavy items by using a yoke, a wooden beam placed across the shoulders so that the weight is evenly distributed and easier to carry. Farmers have placed yokes across the backs of two oxen so that they could work together.

The yoke has been used as a Christian symbol related to the cross. A yoke shows a commitment to work, toward fulfilling responsibilities and following the path toward God.

INRI: Jesus of Nazareth, King of the Jews

The letters INRI are often found on a scroll at the top of a crucifix. These letters stand for the Latin phrase *Iesus Nazarenus Rex Iudaeorum*: "Jesus of Nazareth, King of the Jews."

In the days before Christ's Crucifixion, Pontius Pilate, the governor of Judea, heard people saying that Jesus Christ was their king. That made Pilate so angry that he accused Christ of treason and ordered His death. When Christ was nailed to the Cross, soldiers placed a sign at the top announcing His crime: "And they placed over his head the written charge against him: This is Jesus, the King of the Jews" (Mt 27:37).

IHS: Jesus Christ

The letters IHS form an abbreviation of the name of Jesus as it would be written in the Greek alphabet. As early as the third century, Christians shortened the Name of Jesus, ΙΗΣΟΥΣ, by writing the first three letters. The Greek letter Σ (sigma) is an "S" in the Latin alphabet, resulting in "IHS."

Known as a Christogram, IHS appears on crosses and other religious articles.

Skull and Crossbones

The Gospel of Mark states, "They brought him to the place called Golgotha (which is translated Place of the Skull)" (15:22). When St. Jerome translated the Old Testament from the Hebrew Tanakh to Latin, the word "Golgotha" became *Calvariae,* from which the name Calvary has been derived. Some crucifixes have the symbol of a skull and crossbones to represent the site of Calvary and Jesus' victory over death. Early crucifixes often show a snake at the bottom of the cross to show Jesus' triumph over the Evil One, the devil.

The Ladder

Ancient civilizations, as well as organizations today, have used a ladder to symbolize the climb to a more virtuous life on the journey to Heaven. Plato referred to a ladder when discussing the progression from attraction to deep love. Muslim legend speaks of Muhammad climbing a ladder to Heaven. Saint Bonaventure and St. Francis de Sales used the ladder in their writings to represent spiritual journeys.

A ladder appears on or near many crucifixes to symbolize the path to Heaven. Some religious artwork includes a ladder at the scene of the Crucifixion because Roman soldiers may have used one to top the Cross with a sign saying, "Jesus of Nazareth, King of the Jews." A ladder may have also been used by Joseph of Arimathea and Nicodemus when Jesus was brought down from the Cross. Saint John states, "Joseph of Arimathea, secretly a disciple of Jesus for fear of the Jews, asked Pilate if he could remove the body of Jesus. And Pilate permitted it. So he came and took his body. Nicodemus, the one who had first come to him at night, also came bringing a mixture of myrrh and aloes weighing about one hundred pounds" (Jn 19:38 – 39).

Exterior of the Cathedral of Sts. Peter and Paul in Troyes, France.

Fleur de Lis

When associated with images of Mary or the saints, the fleur-de-lis ("flower of the lily") represents purity. The fleur-de-lis has also been used to represent the Holy Trinity: God the Father, Jesus the Son, and the Holy Spirit.

Detail of stained glass window in the Royal Chapel of the Palace of Versailles, France.

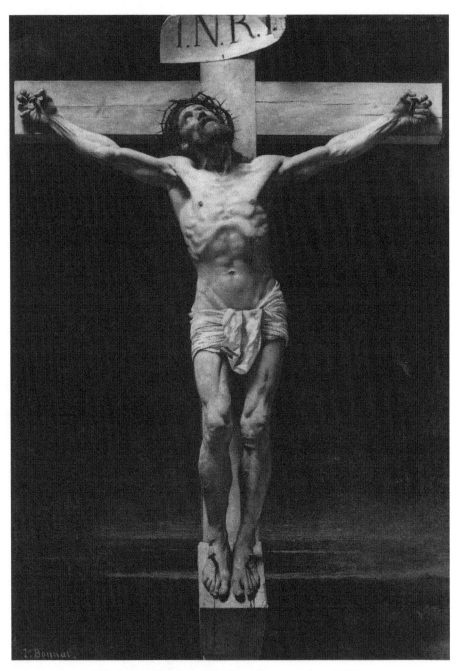

Christ on the Cross, *by Leon Bonnat, circa 1874.*

Birth, Crucifixion, and Resurrection of Christ,
by a follower of Hans Memling, 1510.

Crucifixion

Christians in the 21ˢᵗ century believe the cross is a sign of eternal life. The first crosses, however, signified death.

The ancient Greeks, according to Plato, punished criminals by tying or nailing them to trees or wooden posts. Rulers of ancient Rome enacted the same punishment to scare citizens into obedience. Victims hung on their crosses until they died from starvation, exhaustion, or asphyxiation. This form of public capital punishment was called crucifixion.

Crucifixion comes from the Latin words *cruci* and *fixus*, which mean "fixed" or "fastened to the cross." The word "excruciating" is derived from the tremendous pain inflicted by crucifixion. The horror of crucifixion lessened when Constantine the Great, the first Christian to lead the Roman Empire, abolished its use in AD 337 across an empire encompassing 60 million people.

The Crucifixion, *workshop of Peter Paul Rubens, circa 1610.*

The Y Crucifix

Most crucifixes show Christ hanging with His arms outstretched. In 1610, Flemish artist Peter Paul Rubens painted Christ nailed to the cross with both arms over his head so that His Body formed the shape of the letter Y. Rubens' depiction, *The Crucifixion,* aligns with the view of historians who suggest that Christ may have actually been crucified in that way.[3]

Rubens' painting may have been inspired by the Y crucifixes that were common in the Rhineland area of Germany in the late 13th and early 14th centuries. Known as *Crucifixus Dolorosus* ("painful crucifix"), these portrayed the suffering of Christ in particularly graphic detail.

Crux Gemmata

The first followers of Christ did not use a cross as their symbol because it represented an excruciating form of capital punishment. For them, the cross was an instrument of torture and death rather than something to be honored. In later years, an elaborately decorated design known as the *Crux Gemmata* ("jeweled cross") became popular. A Crux Gemmata has jewels and may be made of precious metals to symbolize triumph over death and the joy of the Resurrection.

Risen Christ Cross

In modern times, the Risen Christ Cross has replaced crucifixes in hospitals, schools, and private homes. This shows Christ, fully clothed, with eyes open and arms outstretched in joy, representing His Resurrection from the dead on Easter Sunday.

While a Risen Christ Cross may be used to bring joy and encouragement, it cannot replace the crucifix that is required on the altar when Catholic Mass is celebrated. In a 1947 encyclical on the sacred liturgy, Ven. Pope Pius XII expressed his displeasure with Risen Christ Crosses: "One would be straying from the straight path … were he to order the crucifix so designed that the divine Redeemer's body shows no trace of His cruel sufferings."[4]

CHAPTER 2

Crosses Used by Catholic Clergy

The Deacon's Cross

Deacons are ordained ministers of the Catholic Church who are either preparing for ordination to the priesthood or planning to remain permanently in the diaconate (members of other faiths, including the Lutherans, Methodists, and Anglicans, also use the term "deacon" to indicate an order of ministry). Catholic deacons do not celebrate Mass but can proclaim the Gospel during Mass and preach, as well as perform Baptisms, weddings, and funeral services.

A deacon wears a cross to symbolize his desire to follow Christ. It often has a sash across it, representing the stole that the deacon wears across his left shoulder, a sign of his ordination.

The Y Cross of a Priest's Vestments: The Orphrey Cross

Vestments worn by Catholic priests can be embellished with an embroidered cross known as an orphrey (from the Old French *orfreis*, meaning "elaborate embroidery"). When worn, the Orphrey Cross looks like the letter Υ because its two arms are placed precisely on the priest's shoulders rather than straight across the back or front of the garment.

Stretching the arms of the cross across the shoulder keeps the design in place as the priest moves about during Mass. It is reminiscent of the Y form of the crucifix in which Jesus is shown with His hands raised above His head.

Any embroidered cross can also be called an orphrey.

Pectoral Cross

A bishop wears a *Crux Pectoralis* (from the Latin *pectus* meaning "chest") on a chain or ribbon so that it hangs around his neck and sits on his chest, close to his heart. When he puts it on, he recites the words "*Munire me digneris*" ("Deign to protect me"), asking God to protect him against his enemies and all evil.

During liturgical functions, the bishop wears the Pectoral Cross over his alb (derived from the Latin word *alba*, meaning "white"), a white ankle-length tunic modeled after the garments worn at Baptism. The priest ties the alb with a belt known as a cincture (from the Latin *cingere*, meaning "to encircle").

Originally, the Pectoral Cross worn by a bishop contained a relic of a saint or of the True Cross, the Cross on which Jesus was crucified. In 1899 the Holy See recommended that the Pectoral Cross of a deceased bishop be given to his successor.[5] In 2020, for example, the Most Rev. Nelson Perez was installed as archbishop of Philadelphia, wearing a Pectoral Cross that retiring Archbishop Charles Chaput had given him eight years earlier when Perez became an auxiliary bishop.

The Bishop's Crosier and the Pope's Ferula

During religious processions, bishops of the Roman Catholic, Anglican, and some European Lutheran Churches sometimes carry an ornate metal or wooden staff known as a crosier (from the Latin *crux*, meaning "cross"; also spelled crozier). At the top there is often a Latin cross or a tau, the T-shaped cross carried by members of the Franciscan Order.

The crosier resembles a shepherd's staff and symbolizes a bishop's responsibility to guide his people as a shepherd watches over his flock. It reminds Christians of Jesus' promise: "I am the good shepherd, and I know mine and mine know me, just as the Father

Pope Benedict XVI holds the ferula of Bl. Pope Pius IX.

knows me and I know the Father; and I will lay down my life for the sheep" (Jn 10:14 – 15).

Although the pope also serves as the bishop of Rome, he does not carry a crosier. Saint Thomas Aquinas explained, "The Roman Pontiff does not use the staff … since it is a sign of limited power, which the curvature of the staff signifies."[6] A bishop is selected and installed in his position by his superiors for a limited time. The pope answers only to God, and there is no limit on his time in service to the Church. Instead of a crosier, the pope carries a ferula (Latin for "rod"), a straight stick capped with a cross at the top.

The style of ferula has varied over the centuries. The ferula that Pope St. Paul VI carried at the closing of the Second Vatican Council on December 8, 1965, departed from precedent because it included the Body of Christ rather than an empty cross. On Palm Sunday 2008, Pope Benedict XVI carried a ferula with a gold cross that had been presented to Bl. Pope Pius IX in 1887. During his 2013 visit to Lampedusa, an island off the coast of Italy where migrants from Africa landed, Pope Francis used a ferula that was made from the boots of migrants.

A Profession Cross of a Woman Religious

Catholic women join religious orders to become nuns (cloistered) or sisters and consecrate their lives to God. Prior to 1962, most women religious wore habits, distinctive garments that included a veil, ankle-length skirt, and a cross that was received when they professed their sacred vows. These garments were an essential component of their identity to the outside world.

During the Second Vatican Council (1962 – 1965), many Catholic Church practices were revised. Several orders of women religious began to wear contemporary clothes rather than their traditional habits, rendering them indistinguishable from laywomen. In 1996 Pope St. John Paul II, following a synod, reminded

women religious that they needed a distinctive outward symbol so that people would recognize their calling and seek their services:

> Where valid reasons of their apostolate call for it, Religious, in conformity with the norms of their Institute, may also dress in a simple and modest manner, with an appropriate symbol, in such a way that their consecration is recognizable.[7]

For many women religious orders today, their recognizable symbol is a Profession Cross worn around the neck. The Profession Cross of each religious order includes symbols with special significance to them.

CHAPTER 3

Crosses in a Catholic Church

The Sign of the Cross

Catholics begin and end their prayers by making the Sign of the Cross. An individual touches his forehead, saying, "In the name of the Father," then touches the front of his body, saying, "and of the Son." Finally, he brings his hand from one shoulder to the next shoulder while saying, "and of the Holy Spirit. Amen." This custom is known as "blessing yourself." Pope Innocent III (1198 – 1216) explained,

> The sign of the cross is made with three fingers, because the signing is done together with the invocation of the Trinity. … This is how it is done: from above to below, and from the right to the left, because Christ descended from the Heavens to the earth, and from the Jews (right) He passed to the Gentiles (left).[8]

The Sign of the Cross has been part of the faith since at least the second century, when Tertullian, a Christian author, wrote,

(1)

(2) IN THE NAME OF THE FATHER...

(3) AND OF THE SON...

(4) AND OF THE HOLY...

(5) SPIRIT

(6) AMEN

In all our travels and movements, in all our coming in and going out, in putting on our shoes, at the bath, at the table, in lighting our candles, in lying down, in sitting down, whatever employment occupies us, we mark our forehead with the sign of the cross.[9]

There are variations on making the Sign of the Cross. Some move from the left shoulder to the right. There is also the "Great Sign" in which one uses five outstretched fingers to represent five wounds that Christ suffered on the Cross (nails driven into both hands and feet, and a spear pierced into His side). The "Lesser Sign" is done with only the thumb.

While the Sign of the Cross is most closely associated with the Catholic faith, it is also done by other Christian denominations including Episcopalians and Lutherans. In his catechism, Martin Luther wrote, "In the morning, as soon as you get out of bed, you are to make the sign of the holy cross and say: 'God the Father, Son, and Holy Spirit watch over me. Amen.' In the evening, when you go to bed, you are to make the sign of the holy cross and say: 'God the Father, Son, and Holy Spirit watch over me. Amen.'"[10]

Ash Wednesday and the Sign of the Cross

Ash Wednesday is the first day of the holy season of Lent, a time in which Christians fast and offer sacrifices to prepare for Easter, the celebration of Christ's Resurrection. On Ash Wednesday, a priest makes the Sign of the Cross on each person's forehead and says the words, "Remember, man, you are dust and to dust you will return" (in Latin, "*Memento, homo, quia pulvis es, et in pulverem reverteris,*" from Gen 3:19), or "Repent, and believe in the gospel" (Mk 1:15).

Palm leaves from the previous year's celebration of Palm Sunday are burned to create the ashes used on Ash Wednesday.

A Crucifix in Every Catholic Church

Every Catholic Church contains at least one crucifix, a cross with the Body of Christ. This is a requirement specified in the *Roman Missal*, approved by the Holy See:

> Likewise, either on the altar or near it, there is to be a cross, with the figure of Christ crucified upon it, a cross clearly visible to the assembled people. It is desirable that such a cross should remain near the altar even outside of liturgical celebrations, so as to call to mind for the faithful the saving Passion of the Lord.[11]

If a Mass, the remembrance of Christ's sacrifice, is celebrated outside of a church, a cross must be present:

> The celebration of the Eucharist in a sacred place is to take place on an altar; however, outside a sacred place, it may take place on a suitable table, always with the use of a cloth, a corporal, a cross, and candles.[12]

Jesus, the Living Lamb, sacrificed Himself for the sins of man. Saint John wrote, "The next day he saw Jesus coming toward him and said, 'Behold, the Lamb of God, who takes away the sin of the world'" (Jn 1:29). Christ is referred to as *Agnus Dei*, the Lamb of God, who triumphed over death. Christ's sacrifice on the Cross is a central part of the Catholic faith.

When discussing Catholic use of crosses and crucifixes, Fr. Kenneth Doyle stated, "St. Augustine (354 – 430) gave the underlying rationale for the use of the crucifix, writing, 'The death of the Lord our God should not be a cause of shame for us; rather, it should be our greatest hope, our greatest glory.'"[13]

The Processional Cross

Masses celebrated on Sundays and holidays usually begin with a procession led by an altar server carrying the Processional Cross (or crucifix). It faces forward to symbolize Christ leading His people. When the procession reaches the altar, the Processional Cross is placed in a stand removed from view, as the focus should be on the altar, with its crucifix (a requirement).

Covering the Cross

Catholics go to church to attend Mass and pray in a sacred place with a crucifix and inspiring statues. During Holy Week, the conclusion of the 40-day season of Lent leading to Jesus' Resurrection on Easter Sunday, crucifixes and statues are hidden from view.

The custom of covering crucifixes and statues originated in the ninth century in Germany. At the start of Lent, a large curtain was hung in front of the altar to hide it from the view of the faithful. The curtain, usually purple or black, was called a *hungertuch* ("curtain of hunger"), because it caused the faithful to hunger to be close to Jesus again.[14] The curtain was lifted on the Wednesday before Easter, "Spy Wednesday," when the priest read the Passion of Our Lord that proclaimed, "And behold, the veil of the sanctuary was torn in two from top to bottom. The earth quaked, rocks were split, tombs were opened, and the bodies of many saints who had fallen asleep were raised" (Mt 27:51 – 52).

Over the years, the practice lessened from covering the entire altar to hiding only the crucifix and statues during Holy Week, beginning on Palm Sunday. The Second Vatican Council in the 1960s decided that the bishops of each country could make the decision for their territory. In the United States, according to the *Roman Missal,* "The practice of covering crosses and images throughout the church from [the fifth] Sunday [of Lent] may be observed. Crosses remain covered until the end of the Celebration of the Lord's Passion on Good Friday, but images remain covered until the beginning of the Easter Vigil."[15]

Simon of Cyrene depicted in Christ Carrying the Cross, *Titian, circa 1565.*

Simon of Cyrene Carrying the Cross

Who helped Jesus in His times of greatest need?

The fifth Station of the Cross acknowledges Simon of Cyrene as the man who helped Jesus carry His cross. Little is known, however, of this historic figure. Simon is mentioned in the gospels of Saints Matthew, Mark, and Luke but not in the gospel of St. John.

After He was sentenced to death by crucifixion, Christ was beaten and forced to carry His cross on a long march. Fearing He would die before they could crucify Him, Roman soldiers called Simon to help.

The gospel of Mark states: "And they forced a certain passer-by, Simon of Cyrene, coming from the country, the father of Alexander and Rufus, to take up his cross" (Mk 15:21).

The gospel accounts do not explain why Simon was in the area or what happened to him after his encounter with Christ. Simon was from Cyrene, a region in North Africa that had a large Jewish population. Cyrenian Jews had a temple in Jerusalem so that might be the reason why Simon was passing by as Christ carried His cross.

Legend holds that because Simon gazed into the eyes of Christ, he converted to Christianity, as did his sons, Alexander and Rufus. This cross-bearer is often referred to as St. Simon of Cyrene, with a feast day of December 1.

Stations of the Cross

Christians reflect upon the most significant journey in history, Christ's walk through Jerusalem, carrying the Cross to Golgotha, where He was crucified. His encounters and the torment suffered along the way are known as the Stations of the Cross.

Immediately after Christ's death, many followers were afraid to visit the site of His Crucifixion and entombment. When Constantine, ruler of the Roman Empire, granted permission for Christians to freely practice their religion in 313 AD, the faithful began making pilgrimages to retrace Christ's steps in Jerusalem. They called their path the *Via Dolorosa* ("Sorrowful Way") and processed approximately one-half mile from what they believed was the location of Pontius Pilate's judgment hall to the hill where Christ died on the Cross.

Most Christians were not able to travel to the Holy Land. To solve that problem, Pope Innocent XI (1676 – 1689) permitted members of the Franciscan Order to erect statues in their churches representing the various moments along the Way of the Cross. In 1731 Pope Clement XII allowed all churches to have Stations, and he fixed the number at 14.

The Stations of the Cross consist of a series of 14 plaques displaying the events of the Passion and death of Jesus Christ. They are displayed around the walls of churches, in outdoor settings, and in some stained-glass church windows. Traditionally Catholics reflect upon the Stations on Fridays during Lent. They walk the perimeter of their churches and stop and pray at each Station. Some Protestant denominations, especially the Episcopalian and Lutheran Churches, also make the Stations a part of their Lenten services.

The Stations of the Cross are as follows:

1. Jesus is condemned to death.
2. Jesus bears His Cross.
3. Jesus falls for the first time.
4. Jesus meets His sorrowful mother.
5. Jesus is helped by Simon.
6. Veronica wipes the face of Jesus.
7. Jesus falls for the second time.
8. Jesus speaks to the women of Jerusalem.
9. Jesus falls for the third time.
10. Jesus is stripped of His garments.
11. Jesus is nailed to the Cross.
12. Jesus dies on the Cross.
13. Jesus is taken down from the Cross.
14. Jesus is laid in the tomb.

CHAPTER 4

Protestant Perspectives on the Cross

Protestant churches usually display a simple cross rather than a crucifix. Some Protestants believe that the Body of Christ on a crucifix violates the Second Commandment, "Thou shalt not have false Gods before you." The Catholic view is just the opposite. As Ven. Archbishop Fulton Sheen reminded Catholics, "Keep your eyes on the crucifix, for Jesus without the cross is a man without a mission, and the cross without Jesus is a burden without a reliever."[16]

The use of a crucifix and religious statues has sparked debate among members of various faiths. Some who oppose such religious articles support their beliefs with a passage from Deuteronomy on the danger of idolatry:

> Because you saw no form at all on the day the LORD spoke to you at Horeb from the midst of the fire, be strictly on your guard not to act corruptly by fashioning an idol for yourselves to represent any figure, whether it be the form of a man or of

a woman, the form of any animal on the earth, the form of any bird that flies in the sky, the form of anything that crawls on the ground, or the form of any fish in the waters under the earth. And when you look up to the heavens and behold the sun or the moon or the stars, the whole heavenly host, do not be led astray into bowing down to them and serving them. (Deut 4:15 – 19)

In Exodus, however, God instructed Moses to build the Ark of the Covenant with cherubim (angels) on either side:

You shall then make a cover of pure gold, two and a half cubits long, and one and a half cubits wide. Make two cherubim of beaten gold for the two ends of the cover; make one cherub at one end, and the other at the other end, of one piece with the cover, at each end. (Ex 25:17 – 19).

Catholics believe that Jesus came to earth and should be shown in artwork and religious articles as a reminder of His sacrifice on the Cross. Catholics do not pray to statues and crucifixes but use them as aids to prayer and as reminders, just as family pictures evoke memories of loved ones.

The Cross and Flame: Symbol of the United Methodist Church

In 1968 the Evangelical United Church and the Methodist Church joined to form the United Methodist Church. The symbol of their unity is a logo of a cross linked with a dual flame. The cross represents devotion to God through Christ; the two flames honor the Holy Spirit's presence, as well as the uniting of two churches.

The Seal of the Presbyterian Church (USA)

> Presbyterians are a discerning people who seek the will of God through reading the Bible, prayer and being in communion with each other and other Christians. But the discernment process has meant that Presbyterians have a long history of disagreement, conflict, schism, and reunions.[17]

This statement by Frederick J. Heuser, executive director of the Presbyterian Historical Society, explains why there are many branches as well as symbols of the Presbyterian Church in the current century.

The Presbyterian Church was established by John Calvin in the sixteenth century. Since that time, many Presbyterian churches have used the Celtic Cross as their symbol. The circle at the center of the Celtic Cross represents eternity and the role of Christ as the center of a believer's life.

While many Presbyterian churches continue to use the Celtic Cross, one group, the Presbyterian Church USA, developed a new symbol in 1985: a Celtic Cross topped by a dove representing the Holy Spirit. At the center of the cross are two lines, which resemble an open book, emphasizing the importance of the Scriptures to the faith. The long lines beneath the book suggest a pulpit, an acknowledgment of the history of preaching in the Presbyterian Church. The flames at the base of the cross form a triangle that honors the Trinity and serves as a reminder of when God used a burning bush to speak to Moses (Ex 3).

The Presbyterian Cross created in the 1980s.

The Moravian Star

In 1409, more than a century before Martin Luther led a reformation of religious practices, John Hus began the Czech Reformation, a protest against the Roman Catholic Church. Hus was convicted of heresy and burned at the stake in 1415, but his followers persevered and organized their own church. They called themselves the Moravian Church because they came from the area of ancient Bohemia and Moravia, now known as the Czech Republic. The Moravian Church has also been known as *Unitas Fratrum* (Unity of Brethren).

The Moravian Church developed a network of schools in the 19th century to serve children whose parents were away from home on church missions. At one of these schools, a teacher explained geometric principles by having his students construct many-pointed stars, which were sent to their parents at their mission assignments. Making stars became a school custom, particularly during the Advent season. Today the Moravian Star is one of the best-known symbols of the church. Its points signify the light of Advent radiating in all directions.

The Crucifix in the Lutheran Church

Although he had many disagreements with the Roman Catholic Church, Martin Luther respected the crucifix as a reminder of Christ's sacrifice. Early Lutheran churches in the United States and Europe had beautiful crucifixes on their altars. Crucifixes can be found today in Lutheran seminaries in the United States.

Episcopal Church

Both crosses and crucifixes can be found in Episcopal churches. Services may be opened by an acolyte or server carrying a processional cross or a crucifix mounted on a pole.

On October 16, 1940, the General Convention of the Episcopal Church in America approved the shield which represents the church. The shield's white field symbolizes the purity of Christianity.

The prominent red cross has two purposes. It is a reminder of the blood shed by Jesus and martyrs, and a red cross on a white field is also known as the Cross of St. George, patron of England, the country in which the Episcopal Church originated. The blue portion in the upper left corner represents Mary, Mother of Christ, and the link to Christ's humanity.

There are nine crosslets on the field of blue which represent the nine original dioceses of the Episcopal Church in America as of 1789. These nine crosses are arranged in the shape of St. Andrew's Cross (Flag of Scotland) to honor Samuel Seabury, the first American bishop who was consecrated in Scotland in 1784.

The Baptist Perspective on the Cross

It is customary to find crosses rather than crucifixes in Baptist churches. According to the General Association of Regular Baptist Churches, "While we want to keep the message of the cross ever before us, we also must keep before us the fact that He did not stay on the cross. Instead we serve a living Savior Who will come for us someday. An empty cross speaks of these realities."[18]

By contrast, every Catholic Church displays a crucifix as a reminder that Christ's sacrifice showed His great love for mankind.

The Jehovah's Witness Perspective

Although they are Christians, Jehovah's Witnesses do not use a cross as they pray. They believe that praying with a cross would be idolatry.

*Major General William Green, Jr.,
U.S. Army Chief of Chaplains,
wears a silver cross on his lapel to
indicate his vocation.*

The Mormon Perspective

Mormons do not have crosses in their churches because they wish to focus upon the life and mission of Jesus Christ rather than His death. By contrast, Catholic churches use crosses and crucifixes to honor Christ's glorious Resurrection.

Mormon chaplains serving in the military wear crosses on their uniforms to indicate they are chaplains, a customary military practice.

CHAPTER 5

Outdoor Crosses and Their Meanings

An outdoor cross upon a hill stirs memories. In medieval times, outdoor crosses served practical purposes. Some were boundary crosses that marked the limits of a parish or town. Others were built to establish a place for preaching sermons, making announcements, or even selling fruits and vegetables. In the days before individual headstones were common, large outdoor crosses stood watch over communal burial grounds.

In 1229 the Bishop of Lincoln told the people of England, "There should be a good and well-built cross erected in the church-yard to which the procession is made on Palm Sunday, unless custom prescribes that the procession should be made elsewhere."[19] Many of those well-built crosses still stand. Their presence signifies strength and faith.

Market Cross in Malmesbury, England.

Mercat Crosses

Standing tall and proud, large stone structures known as Mercat Crosses dot the landscape of Scotland. "Mercat" is a medieval word for "market," and these crosses marked the spot where townspeople once gathered to sell their wares and proclaim news.

Immigrants to Canada and Australia brought the Mercat Cross tradition with them when they established towns in their new land.

A 19th-century reconstruction of Charing Cross.

Eleanor Crosses

Among the most beautiful series of outdoor crosses were the Eleanor Crosses erected by King Edward I of England, circa 1285.

Edward was devoted to his wife, Eleanor, and missed her greatly when matters of state took him away from the castle. During one long separation, Eleanor set off to visit her husband but died in the village of Harby in Nottinghamshire. Devastated by the loss, Edward ordered stone crosses to be built at each site where the servants transporting her body rested between Nottinghamshire and her burial place of Westminster Abbey. There were 12 Eleanor Crosses; three survive, in Geddington, Hardingstone, and Waltham Cross.

Across the English Channel, France's King Philip III built stone crosses to mark the route of the funeral procession in 1270 for his father, King Louis IX, the only French king to be declared a saint.

The original Old Charing Cross in London, England.

A 15th-century illustration of a funeral cross of King St. Louis IX of France.

Atrio Crosses: Faith throughout Mexico

The Mexican landscape is enhanced by Atrio Crosses (or Atrium Crosses), elaborately-carved stone monuments that tell the story of Christ's Passion.

From 1524 to 1572, members of Dominican, Franciscan, and Augustinian religious orders came to Mexico to establish churches and religious education centers. In the courtyards (atriums) of their properties, they erected stone crosses to teach the native people about Christ. The face of Jesus was engraved in the center of each cross. The long bar of the cross contained additional symbols of Christ's suffering and death, such as a spear, nail, and skull.

One of the most famous Atrio Crosses can be found at the Basilica of Our Lady of Guadalupe in Mexico City, near the Tepeyac Desert where the Virgin Mary appeared to St. Juan Diego in 1531.

Celtic Crosses

A Celtic Cross, sometimes called an Irish Cross, has a circle in the center. The design is based upon the solar cross used by pagans to honor Taranis, god of the sun. The oldest examples are found in regions once inhabited by tribes of Celtic people, such as Ireland, southwestern England, Scotland, and Wales. Because the crosses appear to have been built before Christianity came to these regions, they most likely indicated land boundaries rather than religious beliefs.

Although historians dispute its accuracy, an Irish legend holds that the first Celtic Cross was made by St. Patrick (c. 385 – 461 AD) who brought Christianity to a group of Celts known as the Druids. The Druids were pagans who used a large circular stone in their worship.

Saint Patrick is said to have drawn a large cross through the middle of the stone in order to bless it, combining two cultures by representing eternity: no beginning and no end.

Of course, St. Patrick's use of a circle on the Celtic Cross does not imply that the Catholic Church grew out of or endorsed pagan beliefs or practices. A circle is a shape found in many aspects of nature and is not used exclusively by any religion. Catholic communion wafers, for example, are round.[20]

Wayside Crosses

Travelers in Catholic regions of Europe often erected Wayside Crosses on roads or in fields or forests to mark significant locations. These crosses gave directions to travelers and sometimes indicated places where an accident or crime had taken place. Some Wayside Crosses have inscriptions stating who erected them and why.

Drivers in the United States often encounter Wayside Crosses as they travel the highways. Known as descansos, these crosses usually mark the location where someone was killed in a traffic accident. Descansos (Spanish for "to rest") note that a death has occurred and a soul has gone to eternal rest.

Many states prohibit descansos because they are distracting, obstruct a driver's view, or damage public lands.

The Cross Fitché

A Cross Fitché (French for "iron point") has a bottom limb that ends in a sharp point resembling a sword or knife. Pilgrims have carried a Cross Fitché so that they can easily place it in the ground to create an impromptu prayer site or for protection while they sleep along the road. Soldiers carried the Cross Fitché during the Crusades as a symbol of picking up their swords to follow Christ.

A Cross to Bless the Waters

Boys competing to retrieve an Epiphany Cross in Tarpon Springs, Florida.

At first glance, tossing a cross into the ocean seems disrespectful. Orthodox Christians, however, do so prayerfully each year in remembrance of Jesus' Baptism in the Jordan River and the start of His public ministry.

Every January 6 the Orthodox Church celebrates the Feast of Theophania ("God Emerging in Light"). Orthodox Christians gather by the ocean, rivers, or lakes while a bishop or priest prays for the safety of all who travel by sea. He then tosses a cross into the water and young men and women jump in to fetch it. Legend holds that the swimmer who retrieves the cross will have a year of good fortune. The swimmers and observers pray together before and after the cross is thrown into the water. They hold the cross high and celebrate the significance of Christ's ministry.

Many Roman Catholic priests bless the waterways in their area every year in August, near the Solemnity of the Assumption of Mary into Heaven on August 15. They often process with a cross to the water's edge and pray. Tradition holds that this custom began when a bishop was sailing on the Assumption and nearly drowned when his boat was rocked by a fierce storm. He prayed to Mary for help and survived.[21] Today when priests bless the waters, they offer prayers for safe travel.

CHAPTER 6

Wearing a Cross

A cross or crucifix is one of the most popular jewelry items worn by men and women alike. Pope Francis reminds us, however, not to lose sight of its meaning: "The crucifix is not an ornamental object or a clothing accessory — sometimes abused! — but a religious sign to be contemplated and understood."[22]

Concerns about wearing a cross or crucifix also arise regarding the Rosary, a devotional string of beads with a cross or crucifix which Catholics use as they pray. It is common for Rosaries to adorn religious habits or Catholic school uniforms. But wearing a Rosary as jewelry is disrespectful. "If the reason for wearing a Rosary is as a statement of faith, as a reminder to pray it, or some similar reason 'to the glory of God,' then there is nothing to object to," says Fr. Edward McNamara. "It would not be respectful to wear it merely as jewelry."[23]

A farmer, for example, might wear a Rosary around his neck because it would fall out of his pocket and become lost as he worked in the fields. It is common to see a Rosary hanging from the rearview mirror of a car, as a reminder to pray for safe travel, or even draped over a computer monitor, as a reminder to resist temptation.

At Baptism, Orthodox Christians are given a blessed gold cross that their church law requires them to wear at all times. The cross is worn on a chain around the neck and displayed proudly as a sign of Christ's triumph over death.

CHAPTER 7
Saint Helena and the True Cross

The Emperor Constantine legalized the practice of Christianity in the Roman Empire with the Edict of Milan in 313 AD. He proclaimed the faith so strongly that his mother, the future St. Helena, converted. Embracing her new faith, Helena wondered if it would be possible to find the actual cross (the "True Cross") on which Christ had been crucified. She traveled to the Holy Land and supervised excavations on the hill of Golgotha in Jerusalem where Jesus was crucified, and where it was believed His Cross had been buried.

According to legend, Helena found three crosses. To determine which was Christ's, she asked that sick and wounded people be brought to the site. A woman who was near death touched the first two crosses and nothing happened. When she touched the third, she was instantly healed. Helena took that as a sign that the woman had touched the True Cross.

In time, the True Cross was broken up and pieces dispersed around the world as sacred relics. In 1870 Charles Rohault de Fleury, a French scholar, conducted research that suggested that the fragments of the True Cross housed in churches today would be insufficient to make up

Helena of Constantinople *by Cima da Conegliano, 1495.*

or re-create one whole cross. He concluded that Christ's Cross most likely had a volume of 10,900 cubic inches, but the extant fragments totaled only 2,400 cubic inches.[24] One could conclude, therefore, that many fragments of the True Cross have been lost.

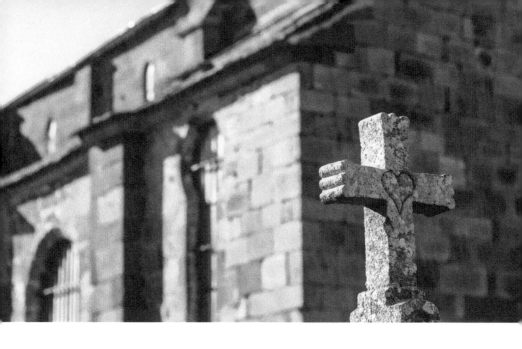

CHAPTER 8
Plague Crosses

Throughout history, crosses have been painted on doors to warn visitors that someone inside had a contagious disease. During the Great Plague of 1665 – 1666, the Lord Mayor of London decreed, "That every house visited [by the disease] be marked with a red cross of a foot long in the middle of the door, evident to be seen, and with these usual printed words, that is to say, 'Lord, have mercy upon us,' to be set close over the same cross, there to continue until lawful opening of the same house."[25]

When a plague struck Rome in 1522, believers prayed in the Church of San Marcello in front

of a wooden crucifix that had miraculously survived a fire three years earlier. They carried that crucifix into the streets and formed a procession that lasted for 16 days. According to legend, the plague came to an end on the last day of the procession, when the cross arrived at St. Peter's Basilica.

Pope Francis re-created that pilgrimage when the coronavirus struck the world. On March 15, 2020, the pope drove to within a few blocks of the Church of San Marcello. He walked the remaining distance as a silent pilgrimage to pray before the miraculous crucifix. Prayers were offered for the sick as well as the healthcare workers who tended to them.

The Sick Call Crucifix

In the days before there was large-scale access to hospitals, most families cared for their sick and dying at home, and doctors made house calls. Priests were summoned when death seemed imminent. When a priest arrived at the home of a dying Catholic, it was customary for the family to meet him at the door with a Sick Call Crucifix.

A Sick Call Crucifix looks like a traditional crucifix, but the top portion slides off to reveal a hidden compartment that holds two candles, a vial of holy water, and a white cloth. The crucifix is placed at the dying person's bedside on a table between the two candles. The white cloth is spread on the table to provide a clean place for the priest to place a pyx, a small container holding the Holy Eucharist that will be given to the dying. The priest uses the holy water to offer a blessing as he administers the Sacrament of the Sick.

CHAPTER 9
Palm Crosses

Palm crosses are made from the foliage and leaves of palm trees that can be found in many parts of the world including Japan, India, and the Americas. They are part of the Easter traditions of many Christians.

Days before His Crucifixion, Jesus Christ entered Jerusalem to the joyful shouts of followers waving palm branches. That event is now celebrated each year as Palm Sunday, the Sunday before Easter. Christian churches distribute palms, which members of the

Faithful raise their palm branches for a blessing in
Parañaque City, The Phillippines.

congregation hold in their hands and wave in remembrance of Christ's arrival in Jerusalem.

Many churches and schools have traditions of the faithful gathering on Palm Sunday to bend or braid the palm to make crosses. The palm is first soaked to soften it for braiding. The crosses decorate homes as well as cemeteries during the Easter season.

Because the palm is a sacramental, having been blessed by a priest, it must be returned to the church or burned, rather than discarded. The ashes from burned palms are used the following year on Ash Wednesday.

CHAPTER 10
Crosses and Crucifixes of Saints and Heroes

Saint Benedict: The Exorcism Crucifix

Saint Benedict, an Italian monk of the late 400s, is known as the father of Western monasticism because he developed wise and prudent guidelines for religious life. His *Rule* remains a model for religious orders to this day. Highlights from his life are depicted on the St. Benedict Medal, which appears in the center of the St. Benedict Crucifix.

The front of the medal has an image of St. Benedict at the center. He holds a cross in his right hand. In his left hand, he lifts a copy of *The Rule*. At the sides are a raven and a poisoned loaf of bread, the latter of which symbolizes the attempts on his life. The words *Crux s. patris Benedicti* (The Cross of Our Holy Father Benedict") are written above the images. Around the edge of the medal are the words *Eius in obitu nostro praesentia muniamur* ("May we be strengthened by his presence in the hour of our death").

The reverse of the medal features a large cross with letters representing the prayer, *Crux sacra sit mihi lux! Nunquam draco sit mihi*

St. Benedict Medal

dux! ("May the holy cross be my light! May the dragon never be my guide!"). The letters CSPB surround the cross to represent the words *Crux s. patris Benedicti. Pax* ("peace") is written at the top.

The edge of the reverse side of the medal has the letters VRSNS-MV-SMQLIVB, a reminder of the exorcism prayer, *Vade retro Satana! Nunquam suade mihi vana! Sunt mala quae libas. Ipse venena bibas!* ("Begone Satan! Never tempt me with your vanities! What you offer me is evil. Drink the poison yourself!"). Because of that prayer and the many stories told about graces received and deliverance from evil, shared by those who have made pious use of the medal, the St. Benedict Crucifix has been called the Exorcism Crucifix and is often used in exorcisms.

The St. Benedict Medal is sometimes also used when giving the blessing of St. Maurus that a priest bestows upon someone who is ill. Saint Maurus was an assistant to St. Benedict and known as a patron of those who are ill. At first, a priest could only give the blessing of St. Maurus by holding a relic of the True Cross. In 1959, the Vatican Sacred Congregation of Rites decreed that a St. Benedict Medal could be substituted because it is often difficult to obtain a relic of the True Cross.[26]

Saint Brigid: The Woven Irish Cross

Saint Brigid (c. AD 451 – 525) lived in County Kildare, Ireland, and was known for her charity and kindness. When Brigid's father became ill, she visited his home. The house had a dirt floor covered with rushes,

Saint Brigid's and Saint Peter's crosses

plant stalks that kept down dust and gave a sweet smell. As she spoke to her father about God's mercy, Brigid picked up rushes from the floor and formed them into a cross that had a woven square in the middle and four arms extending from it. That design became known as St. Brigid's Cross.

Irish homes often display St. Brigid's Cross as a symbol of faith. When placed inside above the front door, the cross is a reminder to pray that members of the household are protected from evil, fire, and hunger.

Although modern-day replicas can be fashioned from metal, a traditional St. Brigid's Cross is made with woven plant materials.

Saint Peter: The Upside-Down Cross

"And so I say to you, you are Peter, and upon this rock I will build my church, and the gates of the netherworld shall not prevail against it" (Mt 16:18). With those words, Jesus revealed that, after His Ascension into Heaven, Peter was to lead the Church on earth on His behalf, as His "vicar" or representative. Peter is the first pope of the Roman Catholic Church.

Christianity was forbidden in Rome, but Peter went there to preach because it was the center of the ancient world and had a large population. Because he would not stop spreading Christ's message, the Emperor Nero condemned Peter to death on the cross. Legend holds

Crucifixion of St. Peter *by Caravaggio, 1610.*

that when Peter told his captors that he was not worthy to die in the same manner as Christ, they hung him upside down.

In honor of St. Peter, an upside-down cross is called a Petrine or St. Peter's Cross. A Petrine Cross does not have a corpus because placing one on an upside-down cross would be a sign of disrespect for Christ and His Church.

Nearly 300 years after the crucifixion of St. Peter, Constantine, the first Christian emperor, granted permission for Christians to practice their faith and supervised the construction of churches in which they could gather. The largest of these churches was St. Peter's Basilica, built on Vatican Hill, the site on which St. Peter was believed to have been crucified.

In 1939 excavation led to the discovery of bones beneath St. Peter's. After much study, Pope St. Paul VI in 1968 indicated that there was a strong likelihood that they were the bones of St. Peter. In 2013 Pope Francis allowed public display of the bones.

Since today's pope is the successor to St. Peter, there are Petrine Crosses in several locations in the Vatican.

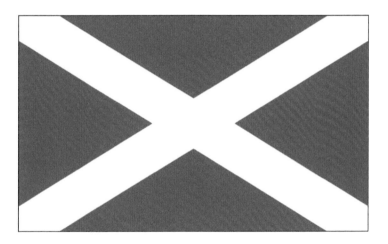

Saint Andrew: The Diagonal Cross

A diagonal cross that resembles an X is called a St. Andrew's Cross, a *Crux Quadrata* ("cross square"), or a *Crux Decussata* ("cross intersection").

Jesus rose from the dead and ascended into Heaven. After the Ascension, His apostles went to many places to spread Christianity. Saint Peter, the first pope, went to Rome, while his brother, Andrew, went to Greece.

Like Peter, Andrew was crucified for preaching Christianity in a land in which it was not permitted. Again, like Peter, Andrew told his captors that he was not worthy to die like Christ. Consequently, Andrew was placed on a cross that was turned diagonally to form an X.

Saint Andrew
by Carlo Crivelli, 1476.

Andrew is known as the apostle to the Greeks. In 1964 Pope St. Paul VI gave a relic of St. Andrew that had been stored in the Vatican to the Orthodox metropolitan bishop of Patras, Greece, the site where Andrew was crucified.

The cross of St. Andrew appears on the flag of Scotland. According to legend, King Oengus II prepared to lead an army of Scots into battle in 832 AD. He prayed to St. Andrew and vowed that he would make him the country's patron if his army was victorious. On the morning of the battle, white clouds appeared to form an X in the sky. The king interpreted that as a sign that St. Andrew would protect the Scots in battle.

The flag of Scotland features a white St. Andrew's Cross (known as a saltire) against a blue background. In addition to Scotland and Greece, St. Andrew is the patron saint of Russia, Ukraine, Romania, Cyprus, and Colombia.

Saint Gilbert: The Portate Cross

The Portate Cross, also known as St. Gilbert's Cross, is slanted to represent a person carrying a cross over his shoulder as Christ did on His way to Calvary. *Porto* is Latin for "to carry" and where we get the words "porter" and "portable."

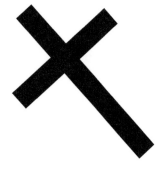

Born circa 1083 in England, St. Gilbert left his wealthy family to live a humble life as a priest. Saint Gilbert suffered from many health problems and struggled to stand erect; his slanted profile is mimicked in the Portate Cross.

Saint Gilbert founded the Gilbertines, the only known religious order of English origin. The Gilbertines disbanded in 1536 when King Henry VIII ordered all Catholic monasteries to close.

Saint George: The Cross of Bravery

Saint George, the Dragonslayer! Dragons might be mythical creatures, but historians believe that St. George was a real Christian soldier born in Turkey circa 270 AD. Because little evidence exists for his deeds, Pope Gelasius I (492 – 496 AD) stated that George is among the saints "whose names are rightly reverenced among us, but whose actions are known only to God." [27]

According to legend, a menacing dragon suddenly appeared in Silene, Libya. As the people cowered in fear, their king demanded that they draw lots and sacrifice themselves to the dragon one by one to prevent him from destroying their land. When the king's daughter drew an unlucky card, St. George appeared. He offered to slay the dragon if everyone in the kingdom would be baptized. Baptisms were performed, and St. George slew the dragon.

Variations of the St. George cross

Artwork throughout the centuries has depicted St. George wearing a white tunic with a bold red cross on the front. A red cross on a white background has become known as St. George's Cross and can be seen on the flags of many nations, including England.

Saint Clement: The Anchor Cross

When early Christians feared persecution, they sometimes used an anchor rather than a cross to disguise their faith. The anchor symbol can be found on Christian tombs in the Roman catacombs. Today the Anchor Cross is also called a *Crux Dissimulata* ("dissimilar cross"). It stands for safety, stability, and hope in Christ beyond this life.

The Anchor Cross has also been named St. Clement's Cross in honor of the martyr who was tied to an anchor and thrown into the sea, circa 110 AD.

Religious Sisters of the Servants of the Sacred Cross wear a pewter cross with an anchor superimposed to symbolize their motto, *Crux Mihi Ancora* ("The Cross Is My Anchor").

Rhode Island has included an anchor and the word "Hope" on its state flag and seal since 1664. It was the first colony to guarantee religious freedom for all its residents.[28]

Saint James: The Cruz Espada

In 844 Abd al-Rahman, caliph of Cordoba, Spain, prepared to embark on a punitive raid against Christians of the north and their king, Ramiro I. Legend holds that on the night before the raid, St. James the Apostle (also called James the Greater) appeared to Ramiro in a dream and declared that the Christians would be victorious. During the battle, it was said that St. James rode on horseback to lead Ramiro's forces in triumph. From that moment, St. James became known as *Santiago Matamoros*, the Moorslayer. Saint James (*Santiago*) is the patron saint of Spain.

The Cross of the Order of Santiago has a red fleur-de-lis design that resembles a sword. The sword represents both the courage of St. James as well as the account that he was beheaded with a sword.

Left: St. James Cross seen on a building facade.
Right: St. Constantine Cross on the Roman Colisseum.

Constantine the Great: The Chi-Rho

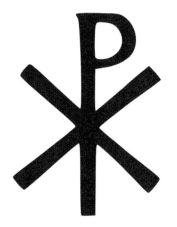

Saint Constantine the Great, the first Christian emperor, was not born in the faith. He was devoted to Sol Invictus, a pagan god of the sun, but his outlook changed on the eve of a battle near the Milvian Bridge in 312 AD. As Constantine and his army prepared for war, they saw an image above the sun that looked like a letter X superimposed on a letter P. Beneath it were the words, *In hoc signo vinces*, meaning, "In this sign (you shall) conquer."[29] Constantine recognized it as the symbol that Christians used to represent Christ. Today it is known as the Chi-Rho or Constantine's Cross. Constantine (now a saint) had the Chi-Rho painted on the shields that his army carried to victory.

Saint Anthony: The Tau Cross

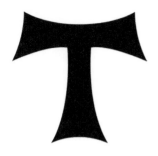

The Tau Cross resembles a letter that appears in both the Greek and Hebrew alphabets. It is one of the oldest and most consistently used religious symbols. The Tau is similar to the mark that the Israelites painted on their doors on the night of the first Passover (see Ex 12). In 1215 Pope Innocent III referred to the Tau at the opening of the Fourth Lateran Council, stating, "We are called to reform our lives, to stand in the presence of God as righteous people. God will know us by the sign of the Tau marked on our foreheads (Ezekiel 9:4)."[30]

The Tau Cross is also known as St. Anthony's Cross due to its association with St. Anthony of Egypt (251 – 356 AD), a pious monk believed to have used a Tau Cross when he prayed alone in the desert. In his later years he founded monasteries in which the monks wore the Tau Cross on their habits. In 1218, men who respected St. Anthony formed a group known as the Brothers of St. Anthony (also known as the Antonines). They wore the Tau Cross when they opened a home for lepers near the town of Assisi, Italy, during the time of St. Francis (1181 – 1226).

Because St. Francis believed that the Tau was a reminder of Christ's death on the Cross, he incorporated it into his signature and even marked his dwelling place by carving a Tau into the walls.

In modern times, the Tau Cross is worn by members of the Franciscan order. The back of the Tau Cross is sometimes inscribed *Pax et Bonum* (peace and goodness), the motto of the Franciscans.

CHAPTER 11

Crosses Associated with Places

The Maltese Cross

The Order of the Knights of Malta was founded in 1048 as the Order of St. John of Jerusalem. Their mission was to protect Christian pilgrims on trips to the Holy Land. Today, Knights (male members) and Dames (female members) of Malta around the world continue to accompany pilgrims to sacred sites, such as Lourdes, France, while serving the poor and practicing works of mercy. In  the United States, they also travel to the National Shrine of Our Lady of Good Help in Wisconsin, the only Marian apparition site in the United States approved by the Catholic Church.

The Maltese Cross has four V-shaped arms, each with two points, forming an eight-pointed cross. It is the symbol of the country of Malta. Ironically, it is not the Maltese Cross but the George Cross that appears on Malta's flag. This is because the George Cross was awarded to the country of Malta in 1942 in recognition of the bravery shown by the Maltese people during World War II.

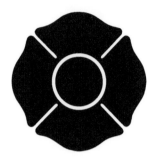

With rounded edges, the Maltese Cross is also the symbol of firefighters, displayed in firehouses around the world. It resembles the cross of St. Florian, patron saint of firefighters. During the Crusades, the Knights of Malta (Knights of St. John) fought the Saracens for possession of the Holy Land. The Saracens attacked with fire, trapping some of the knights and causing them to suffer severe burns. The Knights of Malta became known as firefighters because they rescued their people from the fires.[31]

The Canterbury Cross

Today the Canterbury Cross is a symbol of the Anglican Church. But Canterbury was once the cradle of Catholicism in England and a major pilgrimage site, the place where St. Thomas Becket was martyred in 1170.

In 597 AD, Pope Gregory the Great sent St. Augustine (not the Doctor of the Church and son of St. Monica) to southeastern England to reestablish Christianity in a land in which pagan beliefs were flourishing. Saint Augustine was so successful that he became known as the apostle to England and built a church on the site where Canterbury Cathedral stands today.

The archbishop of Canterbury has been the leader of the Church of England since the sixteenth century, when King Henry VIII broke away from the Roman Catholic Church. Canterbury Cathedral is now the mother church for the worldwide Anglican Communion.

The Canterbury Cross has four arms that extend from a small square in the center. Each arm gets wider as it moves away from the middle. Because they look like triangles, the arms are said to represent the Holy Trinity. The entire cross has a circular appearance that resembles a wheel. It is based on a medieval brooch discovered in Canterbury in 1867. In 1932, copies were made and sent to every Anglican diocese in the world to signify the unity of the church and communion with Canterbury.

The Jerusalem Cross

The Jerusalem Cross consists of a large center cross surrounded by four smaller Greek crosses in each corner. It is believed to have originated in 1099 when it was carried by crusaders who liberated Jerusalem from Muslim rule and reestablished Christianity in the area. For that reason, the Jerusalem Cross is also known as the Crusader's Cross. Its image was used on the papal banner of Pope Urban II's first crusades, which took place circa 1096 to 1099.

The Jerusalem Cross is the symbol of the Equestrian Order of the Holy Sepulchre of Jerusalem, a group that strives to keep Christianity in the area and does charitable work throughout the world.

Throughout history, there have been many interpretations of the symbolism of the Jerusalem Cross. Some believe that the four smaller Greek Crosses on its borders represent the spread of Christianity to the four corners of the earth, or the four directions that the word of Christ spread from Jerusalem. Others feel that the large cross in the center symbolizes Jesus Christ and that the four smaller crosses on the border honor the evangelists: Matthew, Mark, Luke, and John. Another theory is that the total of five crosses stand for the five wounds that Christ suffered on the Cross.

Detail of a fresco featuring a Jerusalem Cross. Northern Italy, circa 1420.

Details of Hill of Crosses,
Lithuania.

Crosses of Lithuania

Craftsmen of Lithuania honor their faith and ancestry by carving crosses and placing them at wayside shrines, churches, market squares, cemeteries, and anywhere people may gather to pray and reflect. The magnificent artistry of the Lithuanian people led UNESCO, the United Nations Educational, Scientific, and Cultural Organization, to include Lithuanian Cross-Crafting on their "Representative List of the Intangible Cultural Heritage of Humanity."

Lithuanian crosses are usually made in the Latin style with rays emanating from the crosspiece. These crosses may have additional ornaments such as flowers, birds, tree of life symbols, or halos. Crosses appear frequently in Lithuanian folk art as well as on the country's Coat of Arms and aircraft. The Order of the Cross of Vytis, a presidential award, has been conferred upon those who have courageously defended Lithuania's freedom.

One of the best places to see the splendor of Lithuanian religious art is at the Hill of Crosses, a pilgrimage site outside the northern city of Siauliai. Pilgrims leave crosses there in appreciation for blessings; as memorials to the dead; to mark weddings and births; to pray for special intentions; and to show that Lithuanians will not hide their Christian

Hill of Crosses, Lithuania.

faith. The origin of the Hill of Crosses is a mystery, but it has been mentioned in writings since 1850, and has withstood times of religious persecution.[32] In 1961, Soviet leaders opposed to Christianity leveled the site with bulldozers, but the faithful continued to bring crosses to the hill. Subsequent attempts to burn the area didn't stop Christians from coming back with more crosses. The Hill of Crosses has flourished since 1991 when dominance by the Soviet Union ended and religious freedom was restored. In 1993, Pope St. John Paul II prayed at the site.

For the people of Lithuania, the Hill of Crosses represents faith, national pride, and the courage to defy opponents of Christianity.

Crucifixes with African Features

Christianity is believed to have entered Ethiopia in the fourth century. In 2019, archaeologists working in Aksum, a region of Ethiopia, discovered the remains of what is believed to be the oldest Christian church in sub-Saharan Africa. Radio-carbon testing suggests that the church was built in the fourth century, close to the time when the Emperor Constantine legalized Christianity in Europe.[33]

Aksum was one of the first regions to use coins for buying and selling goods. The Aksumte Emperor Ezana put the cross on coins, one of the earliest examples of Christian material culture from Ethiopia.[34]

Christianity entered the kingdom of Kongo (now northern Angola) circa 1491 when King Nzinga converted and urged all in his kingdom to join the faith. For roughly the next 200 years, Christianity dominated the land. The Kongo was the site of missionary work by religious orders including the Jesuits (1548 – 1555), Carmelites (1584 – 1588), and Dominicans (1610 – 1612).

The missionaries saw that scepters and staffs symbolized the power of Kongo rulers, so they used a crucifix to introduce Christ as a leader. By the 18th century, the missionaries were gone, but Kongo artists continued to create images of Christ with African features. To people of the Kongo, the cross symbolized the meeting of life on earth with the spiritual world.[35]

Christianity has flourished throughout the African continent. A study completed by the Pew Research Center in 2018 found that Christians in Africa had stronger ties and more dedication to their religion than Christians living in other parts of the world. When surveyed, at least four out of five of the Christians living in Liberia, Senegal, Nigeria, Cameroon, and Chad reported praying daily.[36]

Crucifix by a Kongo artist, circa 16th-17th century,
Metropolitan Museum of Art, New York/Open Access.

The Mount of the Holy Cross in Colorado.

The Mount of the Holy Cross: God Draws a Cross

Men, women, and children have constructed beautiful crosses, but all pale in comparison to the clearly identifiable cross which God Himself seems to have drawn on Colorado's Mount of the Holy Cross. Located in the Sawatch Range of the Rocky Mountains, the Mount of the Holy Cross has a deep inset in the shape of a cross. When the inset fills with snow, an approximately 1,400-foot-high cross appears on the northeastern side of the mountain.

The first documented climb to the cross of snow was made in 1873 by F.V. Hayden, a geologist, and W.H. Jackson, a photographer. Many hikers have since made the climb, often at great peril. Experts warn that only experienced hikers should attempt the trip.

The Mount of the Holy Cross has inspired painters, photographers, and poets such as Henry Wadsworth Longfellow. In his 1879 poem, *The Cross of Snow*, Longfellow wrote:

There is a mountain in the distant West
That, sun-defying, in its deep ravines
Displays a cross of snow upon its side.
Such is the cross I wear upon my breast
These eighteen years, through all the changing scenes
And seasons, changeless since the day she died.

The Mount of the Holy Cross is a reminder of God's presence and promise of protection.

The World Trade Center Cross

A cross brought hope after one of the worst days in American history.

On September 11, 2001, terrorists crashed two airplanes into New York City's World Trade Center, causing the deaths of more than 2,700 people. Father Brian Jordan, parochial vicar of St. Francis of Assisi Church in midtown Manhattan, rushed to the site to comfort survivors and bless the bodies of the deceased. In the devasting days that followed, he continued to visit the scene to minister to recovery workers.

On September 23, 2001, Frank Silecchia, a construction worker from Local 731, showed Father Jordan a cross that was formed when beams of the World Trade Center fell to the ground. As most of the debris from the World Trade Center was being shipped to a warehouse in Staten Island, Silecchia and Father Jordan contacted city officials to save the cross. With the approval of city leaders, volunteer union laborers excavated and installed the cross on a pedestal at the corner of Vesey and West Streets.

For ten months, Father Jordan offered Sunday Masses at the area that came to be known as Ground Zero. Individuals of all faiths attended his services. Because the cross hindered reconstruction work in the area, it was moved to a temporary home outside St. Peter's Church which faced the site of the World Trade Center. It became known as the World Trade Center Cross.

On July 23, 2011, the 17-foot-tall World Trade Center Cross was installed in the newly-constructed National September 11 Memorial and Museum on ground that was part of the World Trade Center complex. Father Jordan blessed the cross again as it moved into its perhaps permanent home.

The World Trade Center Cross as it appeared in the rubble.

CHAPTER 12
Summit Crosses

Those with the bravery and fortitude to climb mountains often mark their achievement by placing a cross at the summit. Summit crosses may be left by the explorers themselves or erected years later to honor heroes, commemorate events, or encourage prayer. They vary from simple wooden branches tied together by a lone explorer to breathtaking sculptures such as the landmark Christ the Redeemer atop Mount Corcovado in Rio de Janeiro, Brazil.

Summit Cross of the Matterhorn

For many climbers, the ultimate goal is to scale the Matterhorn, a mountain in the Alps bordering Switzerland and Italy. The first documented climb of the Matterhorn took place on July 14, 1865. Seven men began that journey but only three survived.

Throughout the years there have been triumphs and tragedies as many have attempted to scale the mountain. At the summit of the Matterhorn is a metal cross to honor those who died in the attempt.

Matterhorn Summit, Switzerland.

Mont Aiguille and Its Crosses

King Charles VIII (1470-98) was so intrigued by the splendor of Mont Aiguille, a mountain in the French Prealps, that he ordered his servant Antoine de Ville to climb it. The servant succeeded in his 1492 journey and was soon joined on the mountain by members of the nobility and aristocracy who planted crosses on the mountain.

The Mount Royal Cross

The Mount Royal Cross is a reminder of Montreal's Catholic roots.

In late December 1642, a sudden winter thaw caused the St. Lawrence River to rise and nearly flood the newly founded colony of Ville-Marie (Montreal), Canada. Paul de Chomedey de Maisonneuve, one of the founders of the colony, prayed to the Virgin Mary and promised to erect a cross on a nearby mountain if the colony was spared.

His prayers were answered, and so he erected a wooden cross on what would later be named Mount Royal.

There are no records to indicate how long that wooden cross lasted or why it disappeared. It was replaced in 1924 with a steel structure that could be lighted to shine down on Montreal.

In 1992, a new lighting system was installed that enabled the cross to be lit in a variety of colors. The cross usually displays white light, but there have been variations such as red for AIDS Awareness and blue for Saint-John Baptiste Day. When a pope dies, the cross is lit in purple and remains purple until a successor is named.

CHAPTER 13
Icon Crosses and Crucifixes

An Icon Cross or Crucifix is one that has pictures to explain events in the life of Christ or the history of the Catholic Church.

San Damiano Cross

Saint Damian (Damiano) was a third-century physician in modern-day Turkey who provided free medical services. Damian and his twin brother, Cosmas, who was also a physician, were martyred in 283 AD for practicing Christianity when it was outlawed during the reign of the Roman Emperor Diocletian.

The San Damiano Cross is named and modeled after one that St. Francis of Assisi admired in the ruins of the Chapel of San Damiano in Assisi, Italy. Thomas of Celano (c. 1185 – 1265), a Franciscan friar and contemporary of Francis, explained:

> Led by the Spirit he went in to pray and knelt down devoutly before the crucifix. He was shaken by unusual experiences and discovered that he was different from when he had entered. As soon as he had this feeling, there occurred something unheard of in previous ages: with the lips of the painting,

Icon of Saints Cosmas and Damian by Jean Bourdichon (1457–1521).

the image of Christ crucified spoke to him. "Francis," it said, calling him by name, "go rebuild My house; as you see, it is all being destroyed."[37]

The experience inside the chapel motivated St. Francis to raise funds to restore the building and continue to spread the Gospel.

The San Damiano Cross, also called the San Damiano Crucifix, has the Body of Christ as its centerpiece. Its uniqueness springs from the detailed illustrations that surround the corpus to tell the story of the Crucifixion. Among the depictions are:

- Mary, the mother of Christ.
- Joseph, the husband of Mary.
- Mary Magdalene.

- Mary, the mother of James.
- The centurion who declared his faith in Jesus.
- The Roman soldier who pierced Jesus' Side.
- The soldier who offered Jesus a sponge soaked in vinegar.
- A small rooster (symbol of St. Peter's denial of Jesus).
- Jesus ascending to God the Father.

Behind the figure of Christ is a stylized crossbar that symbolizes the emptiness of the tomb at the Resurrection. Angels positioned at either side of the tomb gaze upon the apostles searching for Christ.

Good Shepherd Cross of Pope Francis

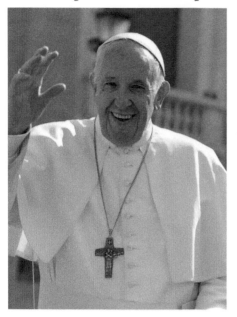 

Most popes receive a new Pectoral Cross when they are elected to lead the Catholic Church. When Pope Francis began his papacy in 2013, he declined a new cross, preferring to wear the silver Good Shepherd Cross that he was given when he became the archbishop of Buenos Aires in 1998.

The Good Shepherd Cross is a reminder of the Scripture passage, "I am the good shepherd. A good shepherd lays down his life for the sheep" (Jn 10:11). In the center is a figure representing Jesus, the Good Shepherd. He carries a lost sheep across his shoulders, as a flock surrounds Him. A dove hovering above represents the Holy Spirit.

The cross was born of a collaboration between a master craftsman and his apprentice. In the 1960s, 15-year-old Giuseppe Albrizzi wanted to become a lathe turner, one who makes and assembles metal components. He went to Milan, Italy, and applied for a job in a factory owned by Antonio Vedele, a craftsman who made religious articles. After many years of working together, Vedele retired and gave his equipment to Albrizzi to start his own business. On one visit to his former apprentice, Vedele sketched a shepherd on a cross.[38]

The Good Shepherd Cross is sometimes referred to as the Vedele Cross.

The Cross of Caravaca

The Cross of Caravaca, named for the town in Spain and the miraculous event that took place there, is a cross with two bars. Christ's hands are nailed to the top bar, unlike most crucifixes on which His hands are fastened to a middle beam. At the bottom are two angels, which face the Image of Christ.

In 1231 Caravaca de la Cruz in southeastern Spain was part of the Moorish kingdom of King Zeyt-Abuzeyt, a leader who did not permit Christianity. According to legend, a priest, Don Gines Perez Chirinos, was discovered preaching Christ's message. The king was curious about Christian practices, so he commanded the priest to celebrate Mass. The priest told the king that he could not say a Mass without an altar, bread, wine, candles, and a crucifix. The king was able to produce everything but a crucifix. Suddenly, two angels appeared and placed a crucifix on the altar. The appearance of the angels convinced the king and his family to convert to Catholicism.[39]

Stanhope Cross

A Stanhope Cross has a magnifying glass in the center through which images of saints or holy places can be seen. The cross is named after Lord Charles Stanhope (1753 – 1816), a British politician who invented an optical lens. Ironically, Stanhope's lens is not the one used in the cross that bears his name. In 1859 René Dagron, a French photographer and inventor, patented a version of the Stanhope lens for use in crosses and jewels.[40]

CHAPTER 14
The Cross of Lorraine

The Cross of Lorraine, also called the Patriarchal Cross, is a two-barred cross with the lower bar being longer than the upper bar. Of all the crosses of the world, the Cross of Lorraine might have the most unusual history. It has been carried into battle by St. Joan of Arc, placed upon the robes of Roman Catholic cardinals, and prominently displayed on — of all things — Oreo cookies.

Historians believe the Cross of Lorraine was first used by Christians in Asia in the ninth century.[41] It became known as the Cross of Lorraine around the year 1099 when Godfrey de Bouillon, the duke of Lorraine, France, made it part of his coat of arms and flew it on his battle flag when he led an army that reclaimed the holy city of Jerusalem from Muslim control.

Saint Joan of Arc and the French Resistance

"An Angel of Deliverance, the noblest patriot of France, the most splen-did of her heroes, the most beloved of her saints, the most inspiring of all her memories, the peasant Maid, the ever-shining, ever-glorious Joan of Arc."[42] That is how Sir Winston Churchill described the young warrior who led the French Army to victory against the English.

Joan was born in Domremy, a village near the Lorraine area of France in 1412, a time when English forces controlled her country. As she entered her teenage years, Joan began to hear voices telling her that God wanted her to liberate France and help Charles, Prince of Valois, become king. At age 16, Joan asked the prince to help her assemble an army. The prince agreed and, in 1429, Joan carried the Cross of Lorraine as she led the French Army to victory over the English at the Battle of Orléans. Later, Joan became a prisoner of the English and was tried as a heretic. Although she insisted she was faithful to God, her opponents believed that the voices she heard were not divine but from the devil. In 1431 she was found guilty of heresy and burned at the stake.

Twenty-five years after her death, Pope Callixtus III concluded that Joan had been tried unfairly and reversed the verdict. She was canonized in 1920.

Saint Joan's bravery and loyalty to France were honored during World War II. Charles de Gaulle's government-in-exile flew the tradi-tional three-color flag of France with the Cross of Lorraine implanted in the center as a reference to Joan of Arc's resistance to enemies of the country.

The Knights Templar

The Cross of Lorraine was carried by the Knights Templar, an organization founded by Hugh of Payns around 1119 and recognized by Pope Honorius in 1129. Making their headquarters in Jerusalem, members of the Knights Templar pledged to abstain from gambling, alcohol, and swearing while maintaining lives of chastity, obedience, and poverty. The Knights Templar protected Christian pilgrims to the Holy Land.[43]

In addition to using the Cross of Lorraine, the Knights Templar also wore on their robes a red cross against a white background.

Freemasons and the Cross of Lorraine

The Cross of Lorraine is the symbol of the Freemasons, a craftsmen's guild believed to have begun in the Middle Ages. By 1717, four Freemason Lodges in London banded together as the Grand Lodge of England. Freemasons could be found in America by 1730.

Today, the Freemasons identify themselves as a philanthropic organization and accept members of every faith.[44] The Catholic Church, however, does not permit its members to join. In an 1884 encyclical Pope Leo XIII explained that the Freemason views on secularism and naturalism conflicted with Church teachings.[45] In 1983 Joseph Cardinal Ratzinger (the future Pope Benedict XVI), reminded Catholics, "The Church's negative judgment in regard to Masonic association remains unchanged since their principles have always been considered irreconcilable with the doctrine of the Church and therefore membership in them remains forbidden. The faithful who enroll in Masonic associations are in a state of grave sin and may not receive Holy Communion."[46]

The Cross of Lorraine and the Crusade against Tuberculosis

Warriors carry the Cross of Lorraine to show that they can stand up to any enemy. Healthcare workers have chosen the Cross of Lorraine as the symbol of their crusade against tuberculosis and lung diseases.

During a 1902 medical conference in Berlin, Germany, Dr. Gilbert Seciron proposed that an organization be established to find treatments for lung diseases. He wanted this new organization to be represented by the Cross of Lorraine: "The red double-barred cross being a symbol of peace and brotherly understanding will bring our message to faraway places. Use it every day as a sign of your combat against tuberculosis and your mission will be successful defeating this uninvited guest that decimates our rows, and thus drying the tears of the suffering mankind."[47]

Today the Cross of Lorraine is used as the symbol of the Canadian and the American Lung Associations and can be seen on the Christmas seals issued to raise funds for research.

Oreo Cookies and the Cross of Lorraine

First produced in 1912, the chocolate wafers of the Oreo cookie underwent many design changes until 1952. Look closely at an Oreo, and you will see a circle topped with a two-bar cross that resembles the Cross of Lorraine. Nabisco, the company which makes Oreos, has not confirmed the meaning of the symbols, although *Or* and *Eo* are Hebrew for "dawn" and light."

Throughout history, the Cross of Lorraine has been carried by soldiers, encouraging them on the battlefield. Modern charitable initiatives have brought Oreo cookies with their Cross of Lorraine to soldiers in military conflicts.

In 2009 Don Martin, senior minister of the Alpharetta First United Methodist Church of Georgia in the United States, sat on a plane next to a serviceman who was returning home after 18 months of service in Iraq. When Martin asked what he missed most while he was away, the soldier immediately answered, "Oreos Double Stuffed."[48] Martin promised the returning soldier that his church would send Oreos to soldiers still stationed in Iraq. This was the beginning of Operation Oreo, a project that sends tons of Oreo cookies to active military personnel as well as veterans in hospitals in the United States. Churches, schools, and charitable groups throughout the United States have joined the initiative by writing encouraging notes to soldiers and sending them to our troops, along with packages of Oreos.

CHAPTER 15
Non-Christian Crosses

The cross has been part of many cultures before and after the birth of Jesus Christ. It is an easily-drawn symbol to which many have attributed meaning.

The Ankh and the Coptic Cross

The ankh, a cross with a loop at the top, symbolizes eternal life. It is most closely associated with Egypt and appears in designs carved into ancient tombs and temples such as the inner sanctum of the Temple of Isis at Philae. New York's Metropolitan Museum of Art has an ankh in its collection believed to have been created circa 1802 BC and placed in the tomb of Ukhhotep or Hapiankhtifi.

The ankh began as a pagan symbol but was adopted by the first Christians in Egypt. After Jesus ascended into Heaven,

The Coptic Cross.

St. Mark, one of the twelve apostles and a Gospel writer, traveled to Egypt to spread Christ's message. By 400 AD Christianity had reached large areas of Egypt and Ethiopia. Early Christians in these regions were called Copts, a term derived from the Greek name for Egyptians. They developed the Coptic Cross, which was largely based on the ankh.

The Coptic Cross is made with two lines of equal length. Each line ends with three points to represent the Holy Trinity of God the Father, God the Son, and God the Holy Spirit.

Swastika

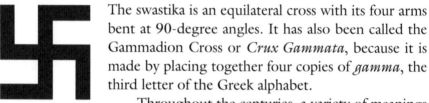

The swastika is an equilateral cross with its four arms bent at 90-degree angles. It has also been called the Gammadion Cross or *Crux Gammata*, because it is made by placing together four copies of *gamma*, the third letter of the Greek alphabet.

Throughout the centuries, a variety of meanings have been associated with the swastika. Interpretations have ranged from good health to the terrible ideology of Nazism — rejected by Pope Pius XI in his 1937 encyclical *Mit Brennender Sorge* (*With Burning Anxiety*) — which gave rise to the horrors of World War II.

Archaeologists found a swastika on a 15,000-year-old figurine of a bird carved from the tusks of a mammoth. Considered the oldest example of a swastika, this carving is believed to represent fertility because the mammoth symbolized that quality. The swastika has also been found on Mesopotamian coins and was used by early Christians as a form of the cross. It appears on Hindu and Buddhist temples, and is used in ceremonies as a symbol of good luck and happiness.[49]

In 1920 Adolf Hitler set a highly offensive and destructive goal for so-called racial purity in Europe. He misguidedly believed in the superiority of the Aryan race, a term used to describe Indo-European, Germanic, and Nordic people. Because the swastika appeared on ancient artifacts of the Aryan people, Hitler chose it to symbolize the Aryan race. The use of the swastika is outlawed in Germany today.

Tibetan Thread Cross

Buddhist monks in Tibet use colored threads to tie two sticks together in the shape of a cross. Tibetan Thread Crosses are considered a way to "trap" evil spirits. The crosses are sometimes hung over the front entrance of a home to prevent evil spirits from entering.

Native American Crosses: Cross in a Circle

Native Americans of the Mississippian Period (1100 – 1541) were spiritual people who used symbols to convey their respect for nature. Artifacts containing the symbol of a cross in a circle have been found in Illinois and other parts of the United States.

Historians are divided on the meaning of the cross in a circle. Some believe that the circle stands for the earth, and that the four points of the cross represent the directions of the compass. An alternative theory is that the circle represents the sun and the four arms of the cross symbolize sacred flames.[50]

Zia Symbol: A Cross of Red

The Zia, a group of Native Americans from New Mexico, used the symbol of a red circle surrounded by red rays that formed a cross. The symbol represented the Zias' respect for the sun and the sacredness of the number 4. They considered 4 to be special because there were four seasons of the year, four directional points of a compass, four seasons of life (childhood, youth, adulthood, and old age), and four parts of a day (sunrise, noon, evening, and night). According to the Zia, "The circle in the middle bounds all of these aspects together in a circle of life and love."[51]

The Zia Symbol can be found on the flag of the state of New Mexico and on commercial products. In fact, because the symbol had been so loosely used on products ranging from detergents to foods, the Zia people sought copyright protection for the symbol in 1999.

The Caduceus and the Rod of Asclepius:
Symbols of the Medical Profession

Two crosslike symbols represent the medical profession: the Caduceus and the Rod of Asclepius.

The Caduceus (Latin for "herald's wand or staff") is a short rod with two serpents wrapped around it, sometimes topped with wings. The Caduceus was carried by the Greek god Hermes (called Mercury in Roman mythology). According to Greek mythology, Hermes was traveling and saw two snakes fighting. He threw a stick at them and they immediately wrapped themselves around it and ceased fighting. Hermes' Caduceus became a symbol of peace, morality, and good conduct, qualities needed by medical professionals.[52]

The Rod of Asclepius is a pole with only one snake wrapped around it. Asclepius (also spelled Aesculapius) was the Greek god of medicine who was said to have healing powers.

Both the Caduceus and the Rod of Asclepius represent the medical profession because Moses used a similar instrument to heal the Israelites:

The Caduceus (top) and the Rod of Asclepius.

From Mount Hor they set out by way of the Red Sea, to bypass the land of Edom, but the people's patience was worn out by the journey; so the people complained against God and Moses, "Why have you brought us up from Egypt to die in the wilderness, where there is no food or water? We are disgusted with this wretched food!" So the LORD sent among the people seraph serpents, which bit the people so that many of the Israelites died. Then the people came to Moses and said, "We have sinned in complaining against the LORD and you. Pray to the LORD to take the serpents from us." So Moses prayed for the people, and the LORD said to Moses: Make a seraph and mount it on a pole, and everyone who has been bitten will look at it and recover. Accordingly Moses made a bronze serpent and mounted it on a pole, and whenever the serpent bit someone, the person looked at the bronze serpent and recovered (Num 21:4 – 9).

Moses' staff is mentioned several times in the Book of Exodus as a tool used in service for good. When his beliefs were challenged by two Egyptian magicians, Moses used his rod to overcome their snakes.[53]

The United States Army Medical Corps began using the Caduceus as their symbol in 1902. The American Medical Association started using the Rod of Asclepius in 1910. Commercial health-care organizations, medical schools, and government organizations use either symbol.

CHAPTER 16
The Cross as an Award

The cross, a symbol of sacrifice, has also become the emblem of valor and bravery. Decorations for valor and distinguished service are often cross-shaped medals or medals that have crosses engraved on them. Whether carried into battle or awarded later for bravery and self-sacrifice, the cross is a fitting symbol for those whose actions benefit humanity.

Pro Ecclesia et Pontifice — For the Church and Pontiff

One of the highest honors the pope can bestow is the *Pro Ecclesia et Pontifice* (For the Church and Pontiff), also known as the Cross of Honor. It is composed of a gold medal with the name of the honor inscribed, as well as a scroll. Established in 1888, the *Pro Ecclesia et Pontifice* can be given to a lay person or a member of a religious community, age 45 or older, who has demonstrated distinguished service to the Church and to the papal office. Past recipients include Paul Salamunovich, an expert in Gregorian Chant; Sr. M. Edward William Quinn, IHM, an educator with more than 50 years of service to Catholic schools; Emile Wijntuin, chairman of the National Assembly of Suriname; Joan M. Kelly, Ph.D., acclaimed catechist and lecturer; and Sr. Julianna Tran, CSFN, who was evacuated from Vietnam during the fall of Saigon and now serves Vietnamese immigrants in the Philadelphia area.

United States Military Crosses:
Distinguished Flying Cross, Navy Cross, Army Distinguished Service Cross.

Military Service Awards

Many nations recognize military personnel who have shown extraordinary heroism by granting awards named for the cross. The United States, for example, bestows three awards of equal distinction: the Distinguished Service Cross for army personnel; the Navy Cross for members of the U.S. Navy, Marine Corps, and Coast Guard; and the Distinguished Flying Cross for aerial flight, including space travel. Here are some of the recipients.

Servant of God Fr. Emil Kapaun (1916 – 1951), a Catholic priest and U.S. Army captain, was awarded the Distinguished Service Cross posthumously, later upgraded to the Medal of Honor. Born on a small farm in Kansas, Fr. Kapaun entered the U.S. Army Chaplain Corps in 1944 and served in India and Burma at the end of World War II. After his military service, he enrolled in the Catholic University of America to earn a degree in education. In 1949, however, he sought permission to rejoin the Chaplain Corps and was sent to serve in Japan.

Servant of God Fr. Emil Kapau and Lt. Fr. Thomas M. Conway.

When North Korea invaded South Korea in 1950, Fr. Kapaun and soldiers in the First Calvary Division found themselves on the front lines of the Korean War. During a fierce battle, Fr. Kapaun's unit was overrun. Rather than fleeing to safety, he stayed behind to minister to wounded soldiers. Father Kapaun was captured by the enemy and spent seven months in a prisoner-of-war camp. While in captivity, he ministered to all and brought hope and comfort to soldiers of all faiths. Upon his death, his fellow soldiers carved a crucifix of spare wood as a way to honor their priest.

In 1993 Fr. Kapaun was named a Servant of God by Pope St. John Paul II, the first step on the road to sainthood.

Lieutenant Thomas M. Conway (1908 – 1945), a Catholic priest and World War II navy chaplain, received the Navy Cross posthumously. A native of Waterbury, Connecticut, Fr. Conway enlisted in the Navy in 1942. In 1944 he became a chaplain of the *USS Indianapolis*, the flagship of the Fifth Fleet. While sailing to Guam, the *Indianapolis* was torpedoed by a Japanese submarine. Upon impact, Fr. Conway and many of the servicemen on board were thrown into the ocean. Rather than seeking his own safety, Fr. Conway swam in shark-infested waters to provide assistance and administer the Sacraments to sailors in peril. Witnesses stated that Fr. Conway's actions likely saved the lives of 67 men. Three days later, the priest died from exhaustion.

*Amelia Earhart receiving her Distinguished Flying Cross medal from
President Herbert Hoover on June 21, 1932.*

At the Navy Cross award ceremony in 2021, Kenneth J. Braithwaite, Secretary of the Navy, stated, "Throughout the brutal war in the Pacific, Father Conway stood by his men and provided comfort, leadership, and spiritual guidance when needed most. I can think of no better example of Honor, Courage, and Commitment. Our Sailors and Marines live those core values every day, and they carry with them the spirit of this great Sailor, officer, and pastor."[54]

Charles Lindbergh received the first-ever Distinguished Flying Cross in 1927. Controversy arose in 1932 when the U.S. Senate voted to award the Distinguished Flying Cross to Amelia Earhart, the first woman to fly solo across the Atlantic Ocean. Members of the House of Representatives disagreed with the decision because Earhart was a civilian, and the award had previously been given only to members of the military for bravery and valiant service. After much debate about her contributions and outstanding representation of her country, Congress approved a joint resolution and Amelia Earhart became the first woman and first civilian to receive the Distinguished Flying Cross.

The Vietnamese Cross of Gallantry

U.S. military personnel have been recognized by other governments for their service abroad.

Servant of God Fr. Vincent Capodanno (1929 – 1967), a Maryknoll priest, was a Navy chaplain who served with a Marine unit during the Vietnam War. He was nicknamed "The Grunt Padre" as enlisted Marines are known as "Grunts."

Father Capodanno was renowned for running on the battlefield to minister in their time of need. On September 4, 1967, he was killed while trying to shield a Marine from enemy gunfire. Father Capodanno was posthumously recognized with the Medal of Honor and the Vietnamese Cross of Gallantry, an award given to show South Vietnam's gratitude to American and Allied soldiers who sacrificed for the freedom of the Republic of Vietnam. His cause for sainthood was opened in 2006.[55]

H. Norman Schwarzkopf, Commander of the Coalition Forces in the Persian Gulf War of 1991, known as "Stormin' Norman," also received the Vietnamese Cross of Gallantry for the bravery he showed as a young soldier during the Vietnam War.

The Victoria Cross

The Victoria Cross of the United Kingdom is one of the most prestigious awards bestowed upon those who show extreme bravery in the presence of enemy forces. While most recipients have been British military personnel, the Victoria Cross has also been awarded to citizens of many countries, including the United States. The criteria is based purely on heroism and can be awarded to civilians or military personnel of any rank.

The award received its name from Queen Victoria, who established it to recognize personnel serving in the Crimean War (1854 – 1856). She personally bestowed the medals on the first recipients, and successive monarchs have followed that tradition.

In 1945 King George VI bestowed the Victoria Cross upon James Joseph Magennis (1919 – 1986), a native of Northern Ireland. Magennis joined the Royal Navy, trained as a diver, and volunteered for hazardous duties on submarine crews. In July 1945 he risked his life in a covert operation by making two perilous dives to attach limpet (magnetic) mines to the hull of a Japanese cruiser. His valor was praised by King George but local officials in Belfast gave him little recognition. It was believed that Unionist city council members did not want to honor Magennis because he was a Roman Catholic. In 1999 he was finally recognized with a statue and ceremony in Belfast. Upon unveiling the statue, Bob Stoker, Lord Mayor of Belfast, stated, "A Catholic hero from West Belfast has been given official recognition at last, nearly 55 years after he was refused the freedom of the city by an earlier Lord Mayor, also a Unionist and an Orangeman."[56]

Although there have been variations, the Victoria Cross usually has the word "valour" engraved under an image of a crown. The reverse gives the name, rank, and unit of the recipient as well as the date on which extreme bravery was performed.

The George Cross

Saint George is the patron saint of England. In 1940 King George VI started the tradition of awarding the George Cross to individuals who display "acts of the greatest heroism or of the most conspicuous courage in circumstances of extreme danger." The award is a silver cross with an image of St. George slaying a dragon.

Like the Victoria Cross, the George Cross is awarded to those who show extreme bravery. The two awards differ in that the Victoria Cross requires bravery in battle while the George Cross does not. As such, the George Cross is usually awarded to civilians, and can be awarded posthumously.

Albert Edward Hemming was not tested on the battlefield, but he showed extreme bravery when, while a section leader in the Civil Defense Rescue Service, enemy rockets struck London on March 2, 1945. Hemming heard a blast and saw his parish church, Most Holy Trinity, in ruins. Fearing for the safety of the church's four priests, Hemming rushed to the scene and began digging through the rubble. Three of the priests were found alive but one was missing. Although the regional commissioner ordered Hemming to move away, he continued to dig, ignoring the smell of gas and the threat that the building might soon collapse. After tunneling nearly 30 feet through debris, Hemming found Fr. Edmund Arbuthnott and pulled him to safety. Both men had serious injuries and were taken to the hospital.

In a rare move, King George VI presented the George Cross to the entire population of the country of Malta in recognition of their bravery during World War II. The George Cross, rather than the Maltese Cross, appears on Malta's flag.[57]

The Episcopal Church Service Cross

Military personnel of the Episcopal faith can wear the Episcopal Church Service Cross next to their dog tags. This cross is bestowed on service personnel by military chaplains or purchased by ministers to be given to members of their congregation as they leave for service.

During World War I, Edith DeWolf Perry, wife of the Episcopal bishop of Rhode Island, designed the Episcopal Church Service Cross for the Army and Navy Commission of the Episcopal Church. She based her work on the ancient Crusader's Cross, the fivefold cross symbolic of the five wounds of Christ at His Crucifixion. She made her design circular so that sharp edges would not hurt a soldier on the battlefield. The front crossbars of the cross have words "For Christ Died for You," based on Scripture: "He indeed died for all, so that those who live might no longer live for themselves but for him who for their sake died and was raised" (2 Cor 5:15).

Among the most distinguished to wear the Episcopal Church Service Cross is Colin Powell, a four-star general of the U.S. Army who attends the Episcopal Church. Powell served the United States of America in many roles including secretary of state, Joint Chiefs of Staff chairman, and White House aide to four presidents.

The Iron Cross / Knight's Cross

The Iron Cross, also known as the Knight's Cross, has been used to recognize exemplary Germanic military service since it was first awarded during the 1813 Prussian War of Liberation. Adolf Hitler honored his military leaders with the Knight's Cross on September 1, 1939, the day German forces invaded Poland.

The Knight's Cross was a black Maltese cross with silver around the edges with, initially, a crown and a royal cypher. Hitler revised the design by adding a swastika. In 1957, a West German statute stated that the Knight's Cross could only be worn and honored with the swastika removed.[58]

Oddly, in the 1960s motorcycle riders in the United States began using the Iron Cross, without the swastika, as a symbol of rebellion against rules. By the early 2000s, the Iron Cross was adopted for use by skateboarders, bike riders, and extreme sports enthusiasts. Noting the widespread use by sportsmen, the Anti-Defamation League issued the following statement:

> The use of the Iron Cross in a non-racist context has greatly proliferated in the United States, to the point that an Iron Cross in isolation (i.e., without a superimposed swastika or without other accompanying hate symbols) cannot be determined to be a hate symbol. Care must therefore be used to correctly interpret this symbol in whatever context in which it may be found.[59]

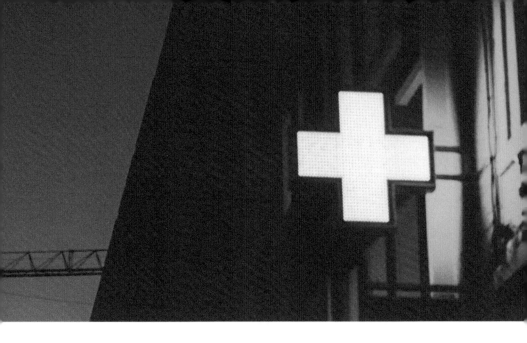

CHAPTER 17
Colorful Crosses

Black Cross

Throughout history, many groups have adopted the symbol of a Black Cross. One of the earliest were the Teutonic Knights, also known as the Order of Brothers, a religious military order founded in 1190. They protected pilgrims traveling to the Holy Land and engaged in charitable work. The Teutonic Knights proudly wore a Black Cross on their clothing and on their shields of armor.

The Teutonic Order coat of arms.

In the 20th century, the Anarchist Black Cross organization used a Black Cross as their symbol but did not give it religious significance. Anarchists do not recognize organized religions or governments.[60]

A Black Cross is also the symbol of the American Black Cross, a volunteer organization that helps underserved communities recover from the effects of hurricanes and other natural disasters.

White Cross

Throughout the world, a White Cross is used to honor fallen soldiers. In the United States, the American Legion, a group that serves veterans as well as active-duty military personnel, places White Crosses on veterans' graves on Memorial Day. Citizens of New Zealand and Australia use White Crosses to honor fallen soldiers on Anzac Day, April 25. Anzac is an acronym for "Australian and New Zealand Army Corps."

A variation of the Polish White Cross logo.

The White Cross was used by a group that provided humanitarian aid to Polish soldiers. Known as the Polish White Cross, the group was formed in New York City in 1918 with a mission to provide health care and other humanitarian aid to Polish soldiers wherever they were stationed. The Polish White Cross operated field hospitals from 1918 to 1946 and sent medicine and supplies to Polish families throughout the world.

In the present century, a small wooden White Cross placed on a lawn has also come to symbolize a life lost to abortion. Churches often display these crosses to represent the number of abortions in the state in which they are located.

Blue Cross

The Blue Cross logo.

Prior to 1900, many people did not have access to hospitals. They had their babies at home and often died in their own homes. By the 1920s, medical care had improved and hospitals had expanded, but costs were often beyond the reach of the average working person.

In 1929 Justin Ford Kimball, vice president of Baylor University's health care facilities, appalled that local teachers could not afford hospital care, developed a plan. He organized a group of 1,000 teachers, each paying $6 a year in exchange for a promise of 21 days of health care if and when they needed it. In 1934, the group took the name the Blue Cross. The success of the Blue Cross paved the way for the other health plans that followed.[61]

Red Cross

One of the world's most powerful symbols of peace, the Red Cross was born on the battlefield.

John Henry Dunant, a 31-year-old businessman, regularly engaged in charitable and religious activities outside of his office hours. He tried to help wherever he could. God gave him an unexpected opportunity when he arrived for a business meeting in Castiglione della Pieve, Italy, on June 24, 1859, as the Battle of Solferino was being fought nearby.

Solferino was a decisive battle in the struggle for Italian unification. French troops, allied to the Sardinians, fought Austrian troops. After nearly 15 hours of fighting, approximately 6,000 soldiers were dead and over 35,000 were missing or wounded.

Dunant watched as casualties overwhelmed the medical services of the army and town. For over three days, he joined the townspeople to care for the wounded.

Horrified by the violence, Dunant believed that the world should unite to offer medical care to injured soldiers of every nation. What seemed like an impossible dream became reality in 1864 when Dunant gathered representatives of 12 nations to form a peace treaty that became known as the Geneva Convention, an agreement that battlefield hospitals, ambulances, and those providing care, identified by a simple, bright red cross, would not be attacked. The Red Cross was reminiscent of Dunant's homeland, the flag of Switzerland with a white cross on a red background.

In 1901, Dunant became the world's first recipient of the Nobel Peace Prize. The International Committee of the Red Cross praised Dunant, stating, "Without you, the Red Cross, the supreme humanitarian achievement of the 19th century, would probably have never been undertaken.[62]

United States Navy hospital ship USNS Comfort

Since 1899, all military hospital ships, regardless of their country of origin or branch of service, have been painted white with red crosses painted on their decks, stacks, or sides so that can be easily identified and protected as caregivers of the sick and injured.

In countries with predominantly Muslim populations, the symbol of a Red Crescent is used instead of a cross. A Red Cross and Red Crescent symbolize help and compassion for people of all religions and countries.

CHAPTER 18

The Cross on Paper

Your work is your prayer. Saint Josemaria Escrivá said, "Great holiness consists in carrying out the little duties of each moment."[63] He believed that even mundane tasks could be offered as prayers. In that spirit, children attending Catholic schools often write a cross (+) at the top of a worksheet, test paper, or composition. The cross signifies that they offer their work to God. Sometimes the cross is accompanied by the initials J.M.J., to ask the Holy Family of Jesus, Mary, and Joseph to bless their work.

Students at the Catholic University of America in Washington, D.C., recall that their professor and television broadcast pioneer, Ven. Archbishop Fulton J. Sheen, wrote a cross and J.M.J. at the top of the chalkboard at the start of every class during his tenure there from 1926 to 1950. He continued this practice during his 1950s television program.[64]

Many saints were known to place a cross on the papers they wrote. Saint Faustina, whose diary encompassed six notebooks, began each notebook with a cross and J.M.J.[65] Saint Francis of Assisi used the Tau Cross in his signature.

Signature with a Cross

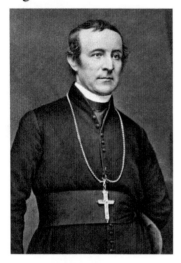

Archbishop John Joseph Hughes.

A cross before or after the signature of a religious leader symbolizes that he is sending his blessing. The custom began during the time when priests were responsible for large territories and were too far away to bestow blessings in person.

One of the most famous to use this symbol was John Joseph Hughes (1797 – 1864), a Philadelphia priest and future archbishop of New York. Father Hughes fought against bigotry and wrote letters to the newspapers when he witnessed injustice. In 1835 John Breckenridge, a Presbyterian minister, challenged Fr. Hughes to a public debate on topics including the role of the pope and the work of Irish immigrants in Philadelphia. Father Hughes suggested they express their views in the newspapers of their respective churches. Since there was no Catholic newspaper in Philadelphia at the time, Fr. Hughes started one. Each week for nine months, the prelates debated each other in print. Father Hughes signed his articles with a cross. That cross and his sharply opinionated views earned him the name "Dagger John," a man who should not be crossed.[66]

Signature of Ven. Fulton J. Sheen.

In the 21st century, only archbishops, bishops, and abbots are expected to place a cross before their names when they sign pastoral letters to members of their flock. Priests, deacons, seminarians, and the laity should not use a cross when signing their names.

Conclusion

The cross is an enduring symbol that evokes a diverse range of beliefs and emotions. For Christians, the cross is a reminder of their Savior, Jesus Christ. To Native Americans, the Zia Cross is a sign of their heritage. The ankh represents life to the people of Egypt and others around the world.

The cross is a symbol of service and hope when used by emergency relief workers of the Red Cross. If victims of earthquakes, hurricanes, and floods see the Red Cross, they know that help has arrived. Cars move out of the way when ambulances marked with the crosses of the medical profession, the Caduceus and Rod of Asclepius, sound their sirens and come to aid the wounded.

A cross becomes a badge of honor when it is worn into battle or bestowed upon a hero. Recipients exemplify the best qualities of humanity and proof that good triumphs over evil.

When displayed on a flag, a cross stirs patriotism and pride. The people of the United Kingdom proudly fly the Union Jack adorned with a cross. There is optimism when citizens of Rhode Island see an anchor and the word "Hope" at the top of their flag.

Kings and queens of Christian nations have worn crowns topped with a cross to show that their authority derives from God, and that they properly reign under obedience to God's moral law. At their coronations, monarchs of the United Kingdom are presented with an orb and a scepter topped with crosses.

The cross has been carried by the faithful in religious processions, soldiers in battle, travelers on pilgrimages, and health-care workers on missions. Worn by rulers as well as the impoverished, the cross is a universal symbol that unites and inspires.

About the Author

Helen Hoffner, Ed.D., is a professor and program coordinator, overseeing the reading specialist program in the School of Education of Holy Family University in Philadelphia, Pennsylvania.

She earned a bachelor's degree in early childhood education from West Chester University; a master's degree in the Psychology of Reading from Temple University; and a doctorate in language arts from Widener University. She has served as an elementary classroom teacher; a reading specialist working with students from ages 5 to 21; the director of a school for students with learning disabilities; and a professor of language arts teaching students at the bachelor's, master's, and doctoral levels. She has written language arts textbooks and is a consultant to the Educational Testing Service (ETS) and 20th Century Fox/ MGM Home Entertainment Corporation.

Her interests include researching the origins of religious traditions and artifacts. She has written two books on the subject, *The Rosary Collector's Guide* and *Catholic Traditions and Treasures: An Illustrated Encyclopedia*.

Notes

1   *The Baltimore Catechism, New Revised Edition* (New York: Benziger Brothers, 1962), cover.

2   Ibid.

3   Rose Eveleth, "Some Visions of the Crucifixion Aren't T-shaped," *Smithsonian Magazine*, Apr. 7, 2014, www.smithsonianmag.com/smart-news/crucifiction-may-not-have-actually-been-cross-shaped-180950403

4   Pope Pius XII, *Mediator Dei*, November 20, 1947, www.vatican.va/content/pius-xii/en/encyclicals/documents/hf_p-xii_enc_20111947_mediator-dei.html

5   Catholic Straight Answers, "Why Bishops Have a Pectoral Cross, Ring, Mitre, Crozier, and Pallium?," https://catholicstraightanswers.com/why-bishops-have-a-pectoral-cross-ring-mitre-crozier-and-pallium

6   The Office of the Liturgical Celebrations of the Sovereign Pontiff, "The Staff," accessed February 21, 2023, www.vatican.va/news_services/liturgy/details/ns_lit_doc_20091117_ferula_en.html

7   Pope John Paul II, Post-Synodal Apostolic Exhortation *Vita Consecrata*, March 25, 1996, www.vatican.va/content/john-paul-ii/en/apost_exhortations/documents/hf_jp-ii_exh_25031996_vita-consecrata.html

8   Catholic Straight Answers, "What Is the Origin of the Sign of the Cross?," accessed February 21, 2023, https://catholicstraightanswers.com/what-is-the-origin-of-the-sign-of-the-cross

9   New Advent, "Sign of the Cross," accessed February 21, 2023, www.newadvent.org/cathen/13785a.htm

10   *Luther's Small Catechism with Explanation* (St. Louis, MO: Concordia, 2017), 27.

11   US Conference of Catholic Bishops, *General Instructions on the Roman Missal*, canon 308, accessed February 21, 2023, https://www.usccb.org/prayer-and-worship/the-mass/general-instruction-of-the-roman-missal/girm-chapter-5

12   Ibid., canon 297.

13   Father Kenneth Doyle, "Why a Crucifix Instead of a Cross? Can Medication Be Used to Help This Condition?," *Hawaii Catholic Herald*, Jan. 8, 2020, https://hawaiicatholicherald.com/2020/01/08/father-kenneth-doyle-why-a-crucifix-instead-of-a-cross/

14   Father Edward McNamara, "Covering of Crosses and Images in Lent," EWTN, March 8, 2005, https://www.ewtn.com/catholicism/library/covering-of-crosses-and-images-in-lent-4938

[15] Philip Kosloski, "Why Do Catholics Cover Crucifixes and Statues during Holy Week?," Aleteia, March 22, 2021, https://aleteia.org/2016/03/19/why-do-we-cover-crucifixes-and-statues-during-lent

[16] Patrick Madrid, "Why Do Catholics Have Crucifixes?," *Boston Pilot*, March 14, 2008, www.thebostonpilot.com/article.asp?ID=6018

[17] F. J. Heuser, "All in the Family: A History of Splits in the American Presbyterian Church," Presbyterian Church (USA), May 17, 2012, www.pcusa.org/news/2012/5/17/all-family-history-splits-american-presbyterian-ch

[18] Norman A. Olson, "Baptists Displaying Crucifixes?," *Baptist Bulletin*, March 2004. www.garbc.org/commentary/baptists-displaying-crucifixes

[19] New Advent, "Cemetery," accessed February 21, 2023, www.newadvent.org/cathen/03504a.htm

[20] Catholic Answers, "Is Catholicism Pagan?," accessed February 21, 2023, www.catholic.com/tract/is-catholicism-pagan

[21] Catholic News Agency, "The Annual Assumption Tradition of Blessing the Sea," accessed February 21, 2023, www.catholicnewsagency.com/news/45474/the-annual-assumption-tradition-of-blessing-the-sea

[22] Hannah Brockhaus, "Pope Francis: The Crucifix Is for Prayer, Not Decoration," Catholic News Agency, March 18, 2018, www.catholicnewsagency.com/news/37998/pope-francis-the-crucifix-is-for-prayer-not-decoration

[23] Father Edward McNamara, LC, "Wearing the Rosary as a Necklace," EWTN, June 14, 2011, www.ewtn.com/catholicism/library/wearing-the-Rosary-as-a-necklace-4581

[24] Thomas Craughwell, "Taking the Measure of Relics of the True Cross," *National Catholic Register*, March 25, 2016, www.ncregister.com/news/taking-the-measure-of-relics-of-the-true-cross

[25] Daniel Defoe, *A Journal of the Plague Year* (1722), January 26, 2013, www.gutenberg.org/cache/epub/376/pg376.txt

[26] The Order of Saint Benedict, "The Medal of Saint Benedict," June 14, 2017, www.osb.org/gen/medal.html

[27] Catholic Apostolate Center, "St. George: What Tales Teach Us about Courage," April 23, 2013, www.catholicapostolatecenter.org/blog/st-george-what-tales-teach-us-about-courage

[28] Rhode Island Department of State, "Rhode Island's Royal Charter," accessed February 21, 2023, www.sos.ri.gov/divisions/civics-and-education/for-educators/themed-collections/rhode-island-charter

[29] Yulia Dzhak, "Battle of Milvian Bridge and Rise of Christianity," War History Online, June 23, 2016. www.warhistoryonline.com/ancient-history/battle-milvian-bridge-rise-christianity.html

[30] Papal Encyclicals Online, "Fourth Lateran Council: 1215," February 20, 2020, www.papalencyclicals.net/councils/ecum12-2.htm

[31] Dallas Firefighter's Museum, "The Story of the Maltese Cross," accessed February 21, 2023, www.dallasfiremuseum.com/maltesecross

[32] Christine Bednarz, "Thousands of crosses cover this eerie hill in Europe," *National Geographic,* Feb. 26, 2018. www.nationalgeographic.com/travel/article/things-to-do-hill-of-crosses-religious-tourism

[33] Andrew Lawler, "Church Unearthed in Ethiopia Rewrites the History of Christianity in Africa," *Smithsonian Magazine,* December 10, 2019, www.smithsonianmag.com/history/church-unearthed-ethiopia-rewrites-history-christianity-africa-180973740

[34] Emma George Ross, "African Christianity in Ethiopia," Metropolitan Museum of Art, October 2002, www.metmuseum.org/toah/hd/acet/hd_acet.htm

[35] Mario Pereira and Kristen Windmuller-Luna, "Kongo Christian Art: Cross-Cultural Interaction in the Atlantic World," Metropolitan Museum of Art, October 30, 2015, www.metmuseum.org/exhibitions/listings/2015/kongo/blog/posts/kongo-christian-art

[36] Joey Marshall, "The World's Most Committed Christians Live in Africa, Latin America — and the U.S.," Pew Research Center, August 22, 2018, www.pewresearch.org/fact-tank/2018/08/22/the-worlds-most-committed-christians-live-in-africa-latin-america-and-the-u-s/

[37] Roch Niemier, OFM, "The Challenge of the San Damiano Cross," Franciscan Media, Franciscan Spirit Blog, May 14, 2020, www.franciscanmedia.org/franciscan-spirit-blog/the-challenge-of-the-san-damiano-cross

[38] Renzo Allegri, "Pope Francis' Cross," Messenger of Saint Anthony, April 11, 2014, www.messengersaintanthony.com/content/pope-francis-cross

[39] Lucien de Guise, "This Miraculous Cross Was Said to Have Converted a Muslim King," Aleteia, March 12, 2021, https://aleteia.org/2021/03/12/this-miraculous-cross-was-said-to-have-converted-a-muslim-king

[40] Collectors Weekly, "Vintage and Antique Stanhopes," accessed February 21, 2023, www.collectorsweekly.com/photographs/stanhopes

[41] University of Delaware, "What Is the Lorraine-Cross?," www1.udel.edu/fllt/faculty/aml/CrossLorraine.html

[42] Winston Churchill, *A History of the English-Speaking Peoples*, vol. 1 (London: Cassell, 1956), 417.

[43] Mark Cartwright, "Knights Templar," World History Encyclopedia, September 28, 2018, www.worldhistory.org/Knights_Templar/

[44] The Grand Lodge of Ohio, "What Is Freemasonry," www.freemason.com/what-is-freemasonry

[45] Pope Leo XIII, *Humanum Genus*, Encyclical of Pope Leo XIII on Freemasonry, April 20, 1884, www.vatican.va/content/leo-xiii/en/encyclicals/documents/hf_l-xiii_enc_18840420_humanum-genus.html

[46] Joseph Cardinal Ratzinger, "Declaration on Masonic Associations," Congregation for the Doctrine of the Faith, November 26, 1983, www.vatican.va/roman_curia/congregations/cfaith/documents/rc_con_cfaith_doc_19831126_declaration-masonic_en.html

[47] University of Delaware, "What Is the Lorraine-Cross?"

[48] North Georgia Conference of the United Methodist Church, "Alpharetta First Showers Troops with Oreos," July 17, 2009, www.ngumc.org/newsdetail/69736

[49] Sakshi Venkatraman, "South Asian Americans Face a Complicated Relationship with the Swastika," NBC News, March 25, 2022, www.nbcnews.com/news/asian-america/south-asian-americans-complicated-relationship-swastika-rcna18599

[50] Native Peoples' Concepts of Health and Illness, "Medicine Ways: Traditional Healers and Healing," National Institutes of Health, National Library of Medicine, accessed February 21, 2023, www.nlm.nih.gov/nativevoices/exhibition/healing-ways/medicine-ways/medicine-wheel.html

[51] See Zia Pueblo, accessed February 21, 2023, http://zia.com/home/zia_info.html

[52] Academy of Medicine of Cleveland and Northern Ohio, *Northern Ohio Physician* 91, no. 6 (November – December 2006): 1 – 3, www.amcno.org/assets/docs/3743_NovDec06.pdf

[53] Ismar Schorsch, "The Staff of Moses," Jewish Theological Seminary, January 24, 2004, www.jtsa.edu/torah/the-staff-of-moses

[54] Secretary of the Navy Public Affairs, "Navy Posthumously Awards Navy Cross to WWII Chaplain," U.S. Navy Office of Information, January 9, 2021, www.navy.mil/Press-Office/News-Stories/Article/2467118/navy-posthumously-awards-navy-cross-to-wwii-chaplain

[55] See Stephen M. DiGiovanni, *Armed with Faith: The Life of Father Vincent R. Capodanno, MM* (self-published, 2018).

[56] Iain Stewart, "The City of Belfast Honours a Royal Navy VC — Leading Seaman James Joseph Magennis," The Victoria Cross, October 9, 1999, www.victoriacross.org.uk/bbmagen.htm

[57] BBC News, "1942: Malta Gets George Cross for Bravery [April 15]," *On This Day, 1950 – 2005*, 2008, http://news.bbc.co.uk/onthisday/hi/dates/stories/april/15/newsid_3530000/3530301.stm

[58] Editors of Encyclopaedia Britannica, "Iron Cross: German Military Award," *Encyclopaedia Britannica,* February 4, 2023, www.britannica.com/topic/Iron-Cross

[59] Anti-Defamation League, "Hate Symbol: Iron Cross," accessed February 21, 2023, https://www.adl.org/resources/hate-symbol/iron-cross

[60] Andrew Fiala, "Anarchism," Stanford Encyclopedia of Philosophy, October 26, 2021, https://plato.stanford.edu/entries/anarchism/

[61] Helen Jerman, "How a Baptist Educator and Businessman's Simple Plan Gave Rise to the Health Insurance Industry," Baptist News Global, November 16, 2010, https://baptistnews.com/article/how-a-baptist-educator-and-businessmans-simple-plan-gave-rise-to-the-health-insurance-industry

[62] Sam McFarland, "A Brief History of an Unsung Hero and Leader — Jean Henry Dunant and the Founding of the Red Cross at the Geneva Convention," International Journal of Leadership and Change 5, no. 1 (October 1, 2017): article 5, https://digitalcommons.wku.edu/cgi/viewcontent.cgi?article=1058&context=ijlc

[63] Opus Dei, "What Does It Mean to Be a Saint? Who Can Become a Saint?," September 28, 2021, https://opusdei.org/en/article/what-does-it-mean-to-be-a-saint

[64] Catholic University of America, "Former Students Remember Professor Fulton Sheen," March 27, 2014, https://fulton-sheen.catholic.edu/at-cua/former-students.html

[65] See *Diary of St. Faustina Kowalska: Divine Mercy in My Soul* (Stockbridge, MA: Marian Press, 1987).

[66] Sr. Elizabeth Ann, SJW, "Dagger John (1797 – 1864)," *Catholic Heritage Curricula*, www.chcweb.com/catalog/files/daggerjohn.pdf

Essential Divine Mercy Resources

Diary of Saint Maria Faustina Kowalska:
Divine Mercy in My Soul

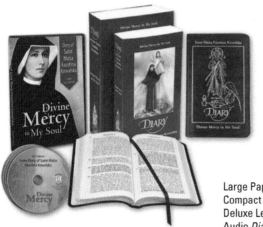

The *Diary* chronicles the message that Jesus, the Divine Mercy, gave to the world through this humble nun. In it, we are reminded to trust in His forgiveness — and as Christ is merciful, so, too, are we instructed to be merciful to others. Written in the 1930s, the *Diary* exemplifies God's love toward mankind and, to this day, remains a source of hope and renewal.

Large Paperback: **Y123-NBFD**
Compact Paperback: **Y123-DNBF**
Deluxe Leather-Bound Edition: **Y123-DDBURG**
Audio *Diary* MP3 Edition: **Y123-ADMP3**

[e] Also available as an ebook — Visit ShopMercy.org

Divine Mercy Catholic Bible

Many Catholics ask what version of the Bible is best to read. In the Revised Standard Version Catholic Edition (RSV-CE) you have the answer.

The *Divine Mercy Catholic Bible* clearly shows the astounding revelation of Divine Mercy amidst the timeless truths of Sacred Scripture. This Bible includes 175 Mercy Moments and 19 articles that explain how God encounters us with mercy through His Word and Sacraments. Leather-bound. 1,712 pages. **Y123-BIDM**

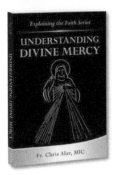

Explaining the Faith Series
Understanding Divine Mercy
by Fr. Chris Alar, MIC

The entire Divine Mercy message and devotion is summarized in one, easy-to-read book! Explaining the teaching of Jesus Christ as given to St. Faustina, *Understanding Divine Mercy* by Fr. Chris Alar, MIC, has it all. Written in his highly conversational and energetic style, this first book in his *Explaining the Faith* series will deepen your love for God and help you understand why Jesus called Divine Mercy "mankind's last hope of salvation." Paperback. 184 pages. **Y123-EFBK**

[e] Also available as an ebook — Visit ShopMercy.org

For our complete line of books, prayer cards, pamphlets, Rosaries, and chaplets, visit ShopMercy.org or call 1-800-462-7426 to have our latest catalog sent to you.

Join the Association of Marian Helpers!

**An invitation from
Fr. Joseph, MIC, the director**

By an act of the Holy See, when you and your family become members of our Association, you'll share in the spiritual benefits of the daily Masses, prayers, and good works of the Marian priests and brothers, just as if you were a member of our religious community!

In addition, you'll receive a specific remembrance in the following ways:

- The daily Masses, prayers, good works, and merits of the Marian priests and brothers around the world;
- A special Mass offered on feast days of Our Savior and His Blessed Mother;
- A monthly Mass on each First Friday and each First Saturday;
- A Mass offered for deceased members on All Souls' Day; and
- The perpetual Novena to the Divine Mercy.

The Marian Fathers of the Immaculate Conception of the Blessed Virgin Mary is a religious congregation of nearly 500 priests and brothers around the world.

Call 1-800-462-7426 or visit Marian.org